GW00750807

Peter Cornwell

success with watercolour

△ The Gardens at Hidcote

Peter Cornwell

shares 25 years experience

of painting watercolours

Published by Bassetts Mill Gallery,
Moat Lane, Chiddingstone Hoath,
Edenbridge, Kent U.K.

Limited Edition: 1000 copies.

FACING TITLE PAGE:

The Gardens at Hidcote 13½ x 9¾ in
Hidcote Manor Gardens are one of the most
delightful gardens in England (quote: *National
Trust Handbook*) about 4 miles north-east of
Chipping Camden.
In the painting the Pampas grass and other foliage
contrasts with the brick pillars and wrought iron
gates. There is no opaque colour or scratching
out. All the whites were protected before painting
began. The people beyond the gates are an
invitation to join them in exploring the gardens.

British Library Cataloguing in Publication Data.

Cornwell, Peter
    Peter Cornwell
    1. Cornwell, Peter
    1. Success with watercolour

ISBN 0-9542287-0-7

Book designed by Peter Cornwell
Colour Plates (copyright) Peter Cornwell 2002
Illustrations (copyright) Peter Cornwell 2002

Peter Cornwell has asserted his right to be
identified as author of this work in accordance
with the Copyright, Designs and Patents Act, 1988.

All rights reserved. No part of this publication may
be reproduced, stored in a retrieval system, or
transmitted in any form or by any means
electronic, mechanical, photocopying, recording or
otherwise, without the prior permission of the
author

Typesetting and origination by TypeStart Digital,
Kettering, U.K.
Telephone: (01536) 418181

Printed in Singapore by Speedprint (Kettering) Ltd.

For Bassetts Mill Gallery, Chiddingstone Hoath,
Edenbridge, Kent.

———————

I dedicate this book to my wife, Pat.

———————

△ At work on a rough sketch: a rare occasion
when the artist was caught sitting down.

Contents

△ **Evening Light** 13 x 9½ in
A scene of contrasting light, on the road between
Groombridge and Ashdown Forest. The warm
colours and long shadows identify the time of
day.

Introduction

Watercolour painting has become an increasingly popular leisure activity. The medium is recognised as difficult to master, but with acquired skills, satisfying and decorative work can be achieved.

This book presents a selection of my watercolour paintings spanning a period of 25 years. Like many who may open this book, I started with limited experience and little training, but a determination to achieve success, sufficient to exhibit my watercolours and acquire a public response.

In this introduction I explain briefly how I became interested in painting, why I chose the medium of watercolour and my personal approach to working with this challenging medium. A commitment to watercolour painting over many years eventually led to establishing a small gallery.

Early interests in painting

As a youngster at school I thoroughly enjoyed the weekly art lesson. Even in those days, freedom of expression seemed to be the rule and there was not much teaching done. Nevertheless using hard-caked poster colours and quite unresponsive paper, the art lesson was a highlight of the week and an opportunity to stimulate my early interests.

I suppose there were half a dozen of us in the class of 20 or so who were keen and we were thrilled when our art teacher had a painting accepted for hanging at the Royal Academy Summer Exhibition. This was something to aim for, to exhibit ones own work.

On Saturdays I had the opportunity to study at the Hornsey School of Art. Regrettably, it seemed that most of my time was to be directed into designing wall paper and curtains. This was not what I wanted to do. I had aspirations to draw and to paint, and would have liked to receive training in watercolour painting about which I knew little. Unfortunately such training was not on offer to part-time students and I had no choice.

Later on, at university, opportunities to paint became fewer, but fortunately my course involved drawing hundreds of zoological and plant specimens, geological sections through rocks, under plane and polarised light and sections through the landscape. All this was good experience, but I did not recognise it at the time.

Other sources of tuition

Opportunities to paint became even fewer during the process of earning a living and bringing up a family and it was not until late in my career when my wife had started to paint again that I took to watercolour seriously. I did not know until then that she also had studied at Hornsey.

With a growing family we spent many pleasant summer holidays painting together. During some spent in Wales and East Anglia, we received tuition. But in my view so-called painting holidays are not suitable for those with serious intent. Tutors are frequently more concerned that you enjoy your holiday than succeed in the art of painting.

I therefore turned to evening classes but found that they were often no better. Tutors were rarely able to spend time with every individual member of the class, and if you seemed to be doing alright you were left alone. However, evening classes did encourage the discipline of painting once a week. It also happened that I was the only watercolour painter among nineteen oil painters and as a consequence I quickly discovered the importance of strength of colour. That proved to be a great step forward in acquiring confidence with my chosen medium.

Had I the chance of receiving individual tuition from a good teacher I would have taken it, for that is unquestionably the best. Unfortunately, opportunities to receive one-to-one teaching of watercolour painting were rare and remain so.

The author

Second best is to teach yourself by extensive reading of the subject and, more importantly, painting watercolour at every opportunity. It is also essential during this process not to be put off by failure and to realise that every attempt is part of the long, slow curve of learning.

There is much satisfaction to be gained. I found that in addition to the reward of becoming fluent with the medium, watercolour painting became a valuable therapy whilst I was involved in a busy commercial career with extensive overseas travel.

My approach to watercolour

I am interested solely in *pure watercolour*, not the use of opaque colour or gouache. I think I was attracted to watercolour, rather than to oils or acrylics because I knew that painting in watercolour was difficult but I was prepared to accept the challenge.

Pure watercolour is the use of transparent washes of colour which allow light to come back through them, off the paper. Good watercolour depends on keeping these washes clean. This is not easy with strong colour, unless the washes are applied in one go, and quickly, with the paper at an angle to let the excess run off. My objective is to achieve *clarity and sparkle* essential to good watercolour paintings best seen from a distance of about 6 feet.

Most artists develop skills and attitudes to painting by looking at other painters' work and by discovering from experience methods that suit them best. Eventually a personal style evolves which they can rightly call their own. You cannot hurry this process. It may take many years for it to happen and the first five are the worst.

Discovering what suits you best applies also to materials. I prefer, for example, to stay with the same brand and quality of paper. For me that is 140lb. NOT (i.e. not hot pressed), usually *Saunders* or occasionally *D'Arches*, as I know from long use how these are going to behave when I apply paint. Bockingford is much more absorbent and as a result gives duller and weaker tones. I strive to achieve good lights in most of the subjects I paint. I prefer a paper that has a moderately hard surface and gives a good, white reflection, rather than one which dulls the light by virtue of a rough grain.

Watercolour painting is a craft and like any other requires the approach of a technician. Progress is achieved by doing it repeatedly and preferably without long breaks in between.

Understanding the behaviour of water

Watercolour technique can be reduced to a few basic skills which have nothing to do with art. The first is to understand how a droplet of water containing suspended pigment, tiny, undissolved particles, is going to behave on a semi-absorbent surface sloping at an angle of about 5–10 degrees. I often apply full brush loads of paint and at any angle greater than this, tones are weakened and it is easy to lose control.

It is unfortunate that water and paper are not good mixers. It is this which makes the process of painting with watercolour so apparently unpredictable and frustrating.

Most watercolour paper contains a small amount of size and this causes water to sit on the surface for quite a long time without actually wetting it. Only after the droplet breaks is it absorbed, and then at an accelerating rate. This has unfortunate effects on the cellulose fibres causing them locally to swell. So if we can understand and handle water on paper the whole painting process becomes a lot simpler. Let's recognise that the water does not contribute anything to the final painting. It is all going to dry off, to disappear. It is just acting as a spreader in an elusive way. Sometimes it has to be given a life of its own and at others kept under tight control.

It is this balance which ultimately produces good watercolour. First think about the water; forget about the paint.

Secondly, having got to know how water behaves on dry paper we need to understand how it will react when a wet brush makes contact with paper which is damp. This is a problem often experienced by the novice, soon to learn that the direction in which the paint will flow depends on the relative quantities of water in the brush and in, or on, the paper; picked up by the brush if drier than the paper, or flow on to the paper if the brush is wetter. This is brought about by the forces of surface tension, the same forces that keep a bubble intact in the air. You do not have to understand the physics, just the effects. It takes time to learn to control what will happen since it is easy to misjudge the dampness of the

paper. Look at it from a low angle. If it is wet it will glisten. If in doubt, touch it with the edge of your little finger. At many stages of a painting it is essential for the paper to be absolutely dry. Be patient and wait!

Getting to know the paint

The third requirement is to understand the paint itself. I avoid using all colours which are stainers such as alizarin. These go into the paper rather than sit on the surface. Most watercolour pigments are discreet particles of more or less commonly occurring minerals. In the process of painting water simply distributes these particles, influencing their density on the paper and in turn influencing tone, soft and hard edges and eventually, when different colours (different minerals) are mixed together, the perceived

Farm buildings at Bassetts Mill

colour. So if you can keep control of the water it should be possible to master control of the paint, that is to say where these particles of colour will come to lie on the paper and eventually adhere. This is ensured by the inclusion of a small amount of gum arabic by the paint manufacturer. Avoiding colours which are stainers and using just those colours made from suspended particles is of great advantage when it comes to lightening an area of a painting or softening an edge. Particles can be readily lifted off with a moistened brush, though some more easily than others. There is nothing technical about this. The ease with which they can be dislodged depends on the size of the particles relative to the pits in the paper, after you have washed out the gum arabic. The fourth basic skill is to understand the way different colours (minerals of one sort or another) are going to react when mixed together, not just the colour they will produce, but how the inherent electrical forces of these different chemicals will cause them to behave. Some will remain as discrete particles on the surface of the paper as a uniform wash, others will clag up in bunches, too heavy to stay in suspension, and start falling out of the applied wash as soon as it comes off the brush. This granulation can produce some very attractive effects. In skies, for example, you can encourage it to happen by combining a very small amount of one colour, acting as a catalyst, with much more of another. Tipping the watercolour painting at different angles while the wash is still wet, or even gently shaking it like a sieve can accelerate the process.

A warning, however, if you want to take advantage of the electrical chemistry: washes in which the particles clag together are more difficult to apply uniformly than those in which the paint particles remain discretely separate. If you look carefully at various paintings in this book you will see how this technique has been used.

The painting process

Whenever possible I like to paint in front of the subject as this gives the work much more spontaneity. You have less thinking time and you have less control. Some would say that this is a disadvantage, but the less you push the paint around and the more you let it flow of its own accord the better the result will be.

I nearly always paint standing up, which means I am painting from the shoulder rather than from the wrist. It gives the application of washes more vitality and reduces the tendency to niggle. Even if I am painting in the studio I still prefer to stand. Remember that washes are going to dry back to at least half their strength, so don't be timid about the strength of colour when washes are first applied. If thought desirable, drop in additional colours or strengthen the tone of a wash immediately after it is applied (the sooner, the safer) and then let the physical chemistry work. If the scene contains rivers or the sea, keep some of the wash in the palette after painting the sky. You may well need it in other parts of the painting.

My paintings are usually half or quarter imperial, sometimes a little less. The size is usually determined by the complexity of the subject and the amount of time I have available, about 3/4 hours for a half imperial and about two hours for smaller ones. This will include a few coffee breaks along the way.

I always stretch my paper before I start, irrespective of size. Watercolour painting is difficult enough without having paper with a mind of its own which cockles to produce rivers of paint just where you don't need them. I rarely paint on to wet paper. Not only do I want to retain strong tones and good lights but I shall almost certainly want to retain some hard edges. So by just touching the paper locally with another wet brush where I want the colours to run provides greater control.

Very often I will stop before the painting is finished and introduce the final touches in the studio. There I will look at it critically and make perhaps half a dozen decisions about parts which should be modified, tones darkened, paint lifted, shadows introduced, leaving other parts untouched and resisting the temptation to over work it.

Painting in the studio

A half imperial painting in which there is going to be considerable detail is best undertaken entirely in the studio. Occasionally the subject is only in my mind or will be worked up from some rough sketches. At other times I use photographs, but in those instances I shall have been to the location and got a feeling of the subject at first hand. I make up my mind about the colours to use independently, often completely disregarding those in the photograph.

▽ **Safe Haven** 11¼ x 8¼ in
A small painting recording details of boats at
anchor on the Norfolk coast, used in subsequent
paintings composed in the studio.

In the studio I can better achieve the quality of
finished work that I want. I think a lot about the
task ahead before actually applying any paint. I
consider what colours I am going to need in the
initial washes and have them all mixed ready to
hand. I use a lot of clean water and brushes to
prevent colours in the palette becoming muddy.
The sky invariably goes in first, hopefully as one
application, reminding myself all the time where
the light is coming from and replenishing my jar
with clean water perhaps every two minutes.
Often I will carry the sky colours down through
the landscape to unify the painting as a whole.
The first 10 minutes or so of actual painting is
usually a frenzy of activity; getting colours on to
the paper in the right strength in the right place,

first time, looking and thinking about what is
happening on the paper all the time, resisting the
temptation to work into wet washes. The edge of
that cloud may not be as soft or as hard or even
quite in the place I want it, but far better to leave
it alone and get the rest of the sky on to the
paper than rescue the cloud.
So at this stage the painting rarely looks quite
what I am aiming for. I have now to let the
physical chemistry happen; the paint has to do its
own thing, the colours to intermix on the paper
and dry back to something like the tones
originally intended. But because other parts of
the paper are perhaps untouched, all glaringly
white, the initial washes will look very strong and
I have to make allowances for that.

When working in the studio it is vital to preserve
the freshness of the painting all the way through.
I may decide that some areas are best masked out
before I start so that the work can progress
speedily. This enables me to obtain coherent
washes without breaking the flow of paint on the
paper, by not having to work round a church
steeple for example. Because I am working in the
studio I may spread the work over two days,
especially if I am a little unsure at any stage about
the way the painting is going. However I will not
complicate matters by starting another painting
before I have finished. I will have put in a lot of
thought and energy to get the painting to this
stage and I shall want to keep all those original
intentions fresh in my mind.

Materials

Pencils, brushes and paper
The following are my own personal preferences;
there are no rules. Artists discover what suits
them best.
For a rough layout of a painting I prefer soft-
leaded pencils (2B–4B) removing most of this
preliminary drawing when the painting is finished
and dry. Harder pencils tend to damage the
paper. Soft ones are easier to remove. I do the
minimum drawing so as not to restrict the
painting process.
My sable brushes are well-worn (Series 33 Winsor
& Newton, Series 3 Cotman and occasionally
Rowney) varying in size from 0 up to 7. A brand
new brush does not produce a better painting
than one which has lost a few hairs and I tend to
use mine until they become impossibly worn out.
For wetting the paper prior to stretching, an old
shaving brush or a mop head brush is useful,
ensuring a gentle touch not to damage the
surface.
The texture and weight of paper is a very
personal choice. Much depends on the surface
texture (roughness) required in the finished
work. Saunders/Waterford 140lb. NOT, already
referred to, has a good consistent quality, not too
absorptive, which stands up well to lifting off
pigment. This quality paper also stands up to
scratching out but if this becomes necessary the
painting has failed!

My palette of colours

Most aspiring watercolour painters like to know what successful artists use, in the belief that working with the same will ensure a good painting. Not so. In fact, for a satisfactory work, tonal values and composition – the considered placement of the subject matter within the limits of the paper – are of far greater importance than colour. Even so, it is not necessary to paint the colours you see in a landscape so often a variety of greens. Be imaginative! Look for the warm and cool colours and accentuate them.

Colour mixing cannot be taught but learned by experience. In my early days with watercolour I painted large numbers of squares with two colours mixed together in different strengths and proportions to build up a reference bank of information. These are still used today. They help me work more quickly. Speed is an essential part of the painting process. Put it on and leave it alone.

I soon learned that if I could not obtain a colour wash from mixing three different pigments I was unlikely to get it from four. Better to start again and use other colours to achieve the desired result. I squeeze my paint onto the commonly sold plastic trays with recesses for mixing. My colours are not arranged in any special order on the palette. The overriding need is to keep the colours clean and dispense with one palette for another as work progresses. I therefore end up with a big washing up session at the coffee break.

Preferred colours

Frequent mention is made in the picture captions of the colours used. Here I identify some of their good and less helpful properties.

The yellows: all of the following can be mixed with blues to give a range of greens.

raw sienna: a warm earth colour, more transparent and cooler than yellow ochre, useful for skies, buildings in sunlight and many other areas of a landscape. One of the colours I use most often.

yellow ochre: another warm earth colour now largely replaced by raw sienna. Yellow ochre is good for painting trees (e.g. oaks in early spring). It needs mixing with plenty of water to give good clear washes.

naples yellow: a favourite of mine: a semi-opaque colour which has a noticeable creamy consistency from the tube and needs considerable dilution to give effective thin washes for sunlit areas and skies.

cadmium lemon: provides sunlight on grassy areas and patches of reflecting mud. Easily dropped into skies for sunlit clouds, but not allowed to mix on the paper too readily with wet blues.

cadmium yellow pale: rarely used; good for harvest scenes when mixed with touches of burnt sienna and occasional inclusion of cadmium orange. This is a strong yellow and for most uses I much prefer cadmium lemon.

cadmium orange: one tube of this pigment will last a life time. It can be over powering and should be reserved for special occasions. A strong pigment which provides juicy greens.

I am not very fond of aurolean or gamboge. I have tried both but have now discarded them.

The reds:

cadmium red: a pillar box red, much preferred to winsor red and crimson lake. Cadmium seems to be more 'reliable' in colour mixes. Good in very small amounts for warming sky washes and makes good mauves when mixed with blues. Provides pleasing strong bark colours with neutral tint.

light red: an excellent pigment for architectural work especially when cooled with ultramarine in the shadows. Transparent if used with care and gives good skin colours when much diluted over dry raw sienna. 'Pretty' when mixed with cobalt blue for skies. Light red and most other earth colours can easily be lifted off the paper surface.

I am not very fond of vermilion or crimson lake, having tried both, but now discarded them along with alizarin.

The blues: I use the four blues: cobalt, prussian, ultramarine and cerulean; sometimes three or all four in one sky painting.

cobalt blue: a clean crisp colour for a clear sky. Tends to be greasy out of the tube, needing thorough mixing with water. Undiluted pigment sticks in the brush. Good for making a range of greys (especially with yellow ochre for the foliage of willow trees).

prussian blue: an exceedingly powerful cold pigment which needs to be very dilute in skies.

Excellent for producing crisp juicy greens when admixed with yellows/cadmium orange and provides deep shadows in lakes and rivers when admixed with umbers and burnt sienna. Too heavy handed with Prussian blue can easily ruin a painting.

ultramarine: an extremely versatile pigment that I use frequently, alone and in mixtures for a range of uses: for good shadows in town paintings when brushed cleanly over dry washes of raw sienna and light red and for shadowy areas and tree trunks in woodland scenes. Ultramarine with other pigments granulates in flat washes. Ultramarine violet can enliven skies.

cerulean blue: a favourite colour for a cold clean winter sky, but apply carefully. Cerulean tends to give unwanted granulation when let run into other wet colours. The coldness and 'brilliance' of cerulean can often be shown up to advantage by juxtaposition with cobalt and/or ultramarine.

The greens: I mix most greens from yellows, umbers and blues. There is no end to the range of cool to warm greens that can be achieved and this is where a reference chart of colour mixes, previously referred to, is most useful. Rarely do I use greens straight from the tube except perhaps Hookers green dark (when I am too lazy to mix one) or viridian, another favourite. This is a clean bright almost iridescent green to achieve a special effect, used just occasionally. Often a landscape is so full of green that it is better to search out the browns, russets and the blues and substitute with mixes of these.

Neutral tint: A small amount is invaluable to produce a muted colour. It works well with cobalt blue and cadmium red, but care is needed not to overdo it, to muddy the mixture. Paynes grey can produce more mud, more quickly than any other pigment I know. I have long ceased to use it and never use black.

△　Springtime in the valley at Bassetts Mill.

Exhibiting

Most people who become interested in painting like to have the opportunity to show their work. By joining an art club or painting group they can judge progress against their peers and have a chance to exhibit in club exhibitions. However, I personally believe that watercolour painting is best done as a solitary activity. Painting alone is preferable to working in groups. To make real progress requires almost unlimited determination and concentration, periods unbroken by distraction.

My wife and I have always been enthusiastic visitors to major London exhibitions and got much pleasure from small private galleries. With confidence in our painting we submitted work to galleries and enjoyed some success, but it became clear with the passage of time that my primary ambition was to have my own gallery in which to exhibit our work. With this in mind we set about looking for a suitable place to live, paint and exhibit; a place where I could retire and spend most of my time building my experience with watercolour.

Bassetts Mill Gallery

After much searching we found Bassetts Mill, an old farmhouse with a barn and granary, set in 12 acres of lakes, pasture and tangled woodland. The Mill had fallen down some 50 years previously. All was neglected and in need of considerable repair. No painting was done during six years' restoration work on the house and the conversion of the barn into a small gallery with studio above. We also reared sheep and made a garden. We started painting again in 1992 and held our first exhibition the following year.

Our gallery has a floor area of some 500 square feet. A headstone at the entrance is dated 1813. The barn has clearly had many previous uses including the keeping of livestock and probably as a grain store. We first used it for lambing and spent many nights sitting with ewes, awaiting new arrivals.

This building, with stone footings supporting brick walls, was built at the bottom of a steep slope allowing water to pour through. This was the first problem to solve.

Planning permission was obtained to install north facing windows for the studio. The entire roof was taken off, lined, insulated and replaced using most of the existing peg tiles. The external stairway to the studio was also rebuilt.

An attractive feature of the gallery is the wealth of original bleached oak beams. The internal walls were panelled to give an even surface for hanging paintings. Panels were also used to cover the internal brick piers to give a three-dimensional hanging space. The walls were then decorated to compliment the soft colours of the stonework and timbers. All of this has retained the ambience of this old building.

Presentation is all-important in hanging an exhibition; in the mounting, framing and positioning of paintings, keeping related subjects together. Well-placed overhead lighting allows the display of some seventy paintings in the gallery.

I believe it is essential to greet all visitors to the gallery with a brief word about the current exhibition and to present them with a professionally prepared catalogue. There is always a bowl of flowers and visitors' book to record all who come.

The complete calm of the location and the unexpectedly professional presentation of the gallery in isolated countryside takes most visitors by surprise. It encourages them to return and recommendations bring additional members of family and friends.

Some 70 people were invited to the first exhibition. There are now well over a thousand active members on the mailing list. The paintings in this book have been kindly lent for inclusion.

By the sea: north Norfolk coast

The coastline between Salthouse and Holme-next-the-sea, some thirty miles of unspoilt scenery, is among the most beautiful in the country. It makes up the North Norfolk Heritage Trust. The area consists of extensive mud flats, ridges of shingle and dunes which provide varied habitats for bird and plant life. It is not surprising that this coast becomes the Mecca for hikers and birdwatchers for most of the year.

Here is brackish and fresh water marshland. Cattle are common in reclaimed areas now isolated from the sea. In places there are areas of pine-wood and scrub land providing a wide diversity of subject material. The low horizons and large open skies are an encouragement to the watercolour painter to lay in loose washes of colour to capture this unique atmosphere.

The topography of the area can be attributed to changing sea levels over thousands of years and to much more recent efforts to manage and reclaim the land by developing protective banks. The roots of sea holly, marram grass and other salt-tolerant plants bind the sand together, encouraging deposits of silt which further help other plants to establish.

Included in this coastline are the villages of Cley, Blakeney, Burnham Overy and Brancaster all of which provide good painting locations. Cley Mill is an obvious and popular subject especially with sunlight on the coloured reeds in the marshland. Brancaster is also one of my favourite locations for both landscape-size and smaller paintings. Here are groups of small boats and areas of calm water.

Behind the coast are the villages of Letheringsett with its small ford, the two Walsinghams (p.62) and Burnham Market, all of which provide interesting diversions when painting the coastline becomes impossible on cold, wet, windy days. For those not familiar with this coast, there is nothing to stop the wind. It can be fierce and bitter even in early spring.

But for the painter who is prepared to work along the coast, the large open spaces and the enormous skies are the principal attraction. I am not sure why the light here seems so different from elsewhere, but it does give this flat, low-lying landscape a simplicity and gentle subtlety of colour all its own. You have only to witness the brilliance of the light coming off the dunes at mid-day to want to capture it on paper.

▷ **Towards Blakeney from Morston**
19½ x 13½ in
Flat marshes with inlets of sea lie between
Morston and Blakeney and when the tide is out
small boats lie tipped this way and that, their
masts at all angles to the sky.
Essential to the atmosphere of this painting are
the clear light, the pleasing sky reflected in the
water and the group of children enjoying a
sparkling summer's day.
Blakeney is a popular resort for painters when
low tide provides the opportunity to capture the
view across these two miles of mud.
To create the impression of distance, I have kept
the buildings sunlit, surrounding them with
darker trees and sky.
The smaller of the two towers is said to have once
provided a guide for sailors.

△ **Norton Marshes** 8½ x 6¼ in
These two paintings of Norton Marshes were
done on the same day. They show the remoteness
of the location. The cottages face Brancaster Bay
but the sea is out of sight still a mile or so beyond
the dunes. Both paintings are treated very simply,
the marshland suggested by just a few vertical
brush strokes.

▷ **Wind off the Sea: Norfolk Coast** 8½ x 6½ in
In this scene, I have tried to capture the effect of
the wind producing a sand haze just above the
horizon and of clouds scudding across an open
sky. The light area in the distance attracts
attention, helped by the low shrubs on the right.
No painting could be simpler; there is nothing to
obstruct the miles of flatness along this coast.

P.B.CORNWELL.

△ **Cley Mill** 13¾ x 9¾ in
This must be the most painted windmill in the country. It faces out to sea almost a mile from the shoreline and, with the surrounding buildings, forms an integral part of this attractive village. Cley Mill was not always so far inland; it is only coastal reclamation which has made it so. Narrow streets with their sharp right-angled bends and the well-known tea shop, bring visitors, especially bird-watchers, to Cley.
I have painted the Mill a number of times, best against a vigorous sky, avoiding the temptation to spell out the sails in too much detail. Lemon yellow, light red, ultramarine and cobalt blue provide the warm reed beds along the River Glaven. The dark trees to the right hold the painting together.

Brancaster at Low Tide 19½ x 13 in

There are many paintable subjects at Brancaster, among them this group of buildings by a small inlet and the boat repair yards not far away (p.24). I stood painting *Brancaster at Low Tide* for 4–5 hours. The tide went out, the small boats became stranded on the mud and the shadows on the white building moved from one side to the other. Experience told me this would happen so I had to decide at the outset what it was that attracted me to this subject in the first place. When I started to paint, at about 11 o'clock, there was strong contrast between the white building and the others behind, their interestingly shaped roofs, the strong directional lines of the reed beds towards the buildings and the reeds themselves with the sun catching the tops. I decided to concentrate on that.The reflections off the muddy banks provided an added bonus as the tide went out. The final brush strokes were put in by mid-afternoon.

Wells-next-the-Sea 9½ x 7½ in
The dominating feature of Wells-next-the-Sea is the green gantry which juts out over the port area. This landmark provides a reminder that the port was once busier than it is today.
I used viridian for the gantry and warmer tones of burnt sienna and ultramarine for the building itself. I have described the new port area of warehouses and cranes in the distance with softer tones. The foreground of the painting is made lively by an assortment of small craft along the jetty.
This is one of the few industrial areas along this stretch of coast. Nevertheless the old part of the town retains its attractions for a lot of visitors to the shops and narrow streets which run down towards the sea.

Still Waters 19½ x 13½ in
With what was left of my afternoon at Brancaster I painted small sketches of boats between the shore line and the dunes further out. The boats were at all angles, some tied to floats, others casually at anchor. The sun was fully out. The light off the dunes and the patches of pale green vegetation formed a strong dividing line between the sea and the sky.
I used this material later in the studio. I wanted to preserve the atmosphere captured in the sketches, particularly the light and the apparent random spacing of the boats. The calm water is restated in the almost perpendicular masts. These are well spaced to give variety to the vertical divisions in the painting.

The Orange Float: Blakeney 20 x 12½ in
Blakeney is a major boating centre. A feature of
this small sea-side town is the long-established
Blakeney Hotel. It is from here that a wide
promontory of sand runs out to sea to end in
Blakeney Point.
The yacht, the principal subject of this painting, is
described just sufficiently to be convincing, with
detail in the rigging reduced to a minimum. But
notice how the water to the left of the yacht picks
up the borrowed colour of the float.
The rest of the painting is simple atmospheric
background; a peaceful sunny afternoon, the sky
painted with washes of cobalt blue and cadmium
red at the top, down through airy clouds of
naples yellow and raw sienna to a haze along the
horizon.
The boats covered by cobalt blue tarpaulins
provide just sufficient interest to balance the
main subject.

▷ **The Green Boat** 12¼ x 8¾ in
This is a studio painting which makes use of sketches made on painting days on the Norfolk coast. It is an imaginary location. The water provides almost mirror images of the boats and buildings. The overcast sky of layered washes suggests a very calm day.
The small bits of debris and stones in the foreground are understated to suggest that the water is turning over very gently. The green boat and the two boatmen redirect the viewer away from the right of the painting towards the buildings.

△ **Quiet Backwater: Burnham Overy Staithe**
9½ x 7 in
Along much of the north Norfolk coast the shoreline consists of small inlets and sand banks. At Burnham Overy Staithe there is an old sea-defence of weathered timbers and cleaved stones worn by high tides, old gnarled posts long-bleached by the sun, pieces of rope used for tying up, rusting cables and chains with great iron rings secured into the sand. All provide detail for the painter. There is enough here for many visits. On this particular summer afternoon it is calm. Two small boats lie idly in the water. The tree on the far bank, conveniently there to balance the composition, is unfortunately now gone, probably lost in a winter storm.

▷ **North Norfolk Coast** 14¾ x 10⅛ in
I must admit to not knowing exactly where this scene is. My wife and I motored from Suffolk along the coast road towards Kings Lynn. We had got most of the way, through some very paintable landscape, and turned down a track leading to the sea. This opportunity was too good to miss. Looking back inland the hills were in part shadow. The dried grass, bleached by the wind and sun, was much lighter than the sky. Pools of brackish water lay in the foreground. A small tower was in the middle distance. Putting all these components together gave rise to this watercolour. In about an hour and a half we were back on our way.

P.B.CORNWELL.

23

Brancaster Boat Yard 18¾ x 12½ in

Standing at an easel on a cold blustery afternoon is not the easiest way to produce a good watercolour. After two to three hours you find yourself moving about to keep warm or huddled up behind a gorse bush for cover.

I have painted this scene a number of times. Not much seems to go on here, but I like it for the dilapidated brick and corrugated iron workshops, the cylindrical fuel tanks and the assortment of boats, some of which appear to have been here for a long time.

Despite the wind, the painting is full of sunshine. The buildings are set against a blustery sky, the one with the viridian green roof being given prominence against the other warmer colours in the painting.

Other coastal locations

In this section I have brought together paintings from many locations; the chalk cliffs along the Channel coast at Birling Gap, the area around Tenby in South Wales and marine subjects at Rhos-on-Sea and Caernarfon on the North Wales coast. I have also included paintings from Lyme Regis in Dorset and from overseas; Jersey, Lanzarote and Fiji. They vary widely in subject matter, but I must admit I like painting the atmosphere of small ports, with brightly coloured boats and all the paraphernalia that goes with the activity of fishing.

These scenes also provide an opportunity to include people, both as the principal subject and as small accents in a painting; holiday makers, sailors tending their boats or generally standing about where some human interest is needed in the composition.

Beaches also provide good material for watercolours; especially pools of shallow water left by the tide and reflecting the sky, patches of wet mud, sea weed and the vegetation of brackish areas. Here are delightful patterns of light and shadow and an abundance of subjects related to securing boats such as ropes, chains and anchors, items of fishing tackle and the ubiquitous rowing boat. They lie at all angles to the beach and the sun and need keen observation and careful drawing to get their shapes right.

◁ **Going to the Beach** 10 x 7¼ in
This scene is a mile or so west of Tenby. It was the house that took my attention with all the compositional lines leading to it, especially when two small boys came walking into my painting. This gave yet more emphasis to the road and fence leading down to the beach.

I liked the afternoon sun top-lighting the headland. It was also striking the gable ends of the building and giving texture to the rough grass.

I decided to strengthen the foreground by putting shadows on the road, thus helping the eye to jump directly to where all the other lines in the painting were going.

25

Tenby Harbour 13½ x 10 in
This is an almost surreal painting of Tenby harbour. The buildings are reduced to simple rectangular shapes, the curve of the harbour wall is much exaggerated and the small boats are simple patches of colour.

I decided to emphasise both the shadows and the reflections and to challenge the overall blue with the bright red roof of the lifeboat station and with the pinks, mauves, yellows and greens of the buildings and trees.

The distant people, no more than spots of colour,

and the nearby chimneys emphasise the extremes of distance in the subject.

Tenby is a busy holiday location, ideal for those who like a harbour atmosphere. It also provides an excellent base for exploring the many bays and sandy beaches of the Gower peninsular.

▽ **The Beach at Birling Gap** 19¼ x 13¾ in

Birling Gap is about two miles west of Beachy Head. It is where the South Downs meet the sea. The high white cliffs are characteristic of much of the south east coast.

I had come to Birling Gap without intending to paint, but after 10 minutes I had borrowed a pencil and some paper from the café on the cliff to produce a rough sketch with colour notes for future reference.

I have made three paintings of this subject but I like this one the best. The succession of the cliffs towards Seaford Head some three miles away seems to work well. Much of the cliffs is left as white paper with only the lightest touches of colour to pick up the sun. The flinty nature of the chalk is hinted at towards the bottom right, together with the accumulation of debris along the cliff bottom.

The pattern of seaweed and stones on the beach, faithfully recorded in the original sketch, is especially pleasing. This pattern is formed in a repetitive and precise way by outgoing tides. The one or two people on the beach, just hinted at, provide scale.

P.B. CORNWELL

△ **Early Morning: Rhos-on-Sea** 13½ x 10 in
Rhos-on-Sea is a small resort on the north coast of Wales and a dormitory town for Llandudno and Conwy. I collected the material for this painting when I walked down to the local newsagent to pick up my morning paper.
This scene is painted against the light at about 8 o'clock in the morning. The sun has risen just enough to give warmth and colour to the beach and jetty. Much of the sea and sky is untouched white paper.

The direction of the light has thrown the foreground into sharp relief. The stones and seaweed are painted in yellows, browns and greens, mixes of prussian blue and umbers. These are surrounded with pools of light which heighten the drama.

The men carrying the boat were caught in a succession of photographs to ensure that in the final painting they looked as though "they were doing a job of work". The principal lines in the composition reinforce where the boat is being taken.

Lyme Bay from Lyme Regis 20½ x 13¾ in

This is the first of three paintings of this south coast fishing and holiday resort. The old customs houses at the end of the cob are now used to house a marine aquarium.

The cob itself is an imposing structure, featured in the novel *The French Lieutenant's Woman*. During the summer, holiday makers often stand watching artists working away at their easels.

Apart from the sea and extensive beach the other attraction is fossil-hunting; the cliff shales at Lyme Regis are well-known for their prolific ammonite content.

My painting contains a lot of detail; the ladders down the side of the jetty exposed at low tide, the red fishing boat moored at the harbour entrance and the buildings themselves, painted in

a range of colour mixes. Burnt sienna, cobalt blue, ultramarine, lemon yellow and raw sienna are all allowed to work together to convey the wet sea weed and other marine growth clinging to the jetty wall. Note the little white dinghy at the extreme right which stops the strong horizontals taking the eye out of the painting. All this contrasts with the quiet open sea and the distant cliffs at Charmouth well into the distance.

△ **Girl with a Red Scarf** 22 x 14 in
I don't often paint close-ups of people. This one is based on sketches made on various holidays where there is little else to draw but that immediately around you.

The girl is placed on the golden section which immediately gives her a strong presence. As the principal character, she is in direct sunlight, the others in shade.

I enjoyed painting the umbrellas, open, closed, from above and below, tilted this way and that. The triangle of reds, the scarf, the girl's towel and the deck chair define a quiet open space in the centre of the painting. But the reds also enhance the green umbrellas grouped around the principal character.

All this is happening under a summer sky. I hope it stays like this all week!

The Old Custom's House: Lyme Regis
20½ x 13¾ in
Another painting of this subject is on p.29. Here
at the end of the cob the buildings are painted in
three dimensions, light on one side and the gable
end in shadow. Most of the lines in this
composition, the coping stones running up from
the right and the steps up from the beach, lead
directly to the buildings and groups of people.
There is a lot going on in the middle distance and
in the treatment of the foreground stonework; the
sea-washed timbers, the tyre on the beach and the
red charity box further up the quay. The sea gulls
on the roof provide a further touch of
authenticity. These details make the viewer believe
he is there.

△ **Low Tide: Jersey** 14¾ x 9¾ in
The boat in this painting was sketched in pencil paying particular attention to detail.
The viewer is caught within the composition. First the eye is attracted to the boat, then to the small group of people and boats by the steps and finally the viewer is allowed to escape beyond the cliff face and out to the horizon. But the gully in the beach directs attention back, to look again at the green boat and its attractive features.

▷ **Caernarfon from Anglese**y 13¾ x 11 in
Over the Menai bridge, turn left and there is the village of Brynsieneyn. Down towards the coast, Liandian provides a good viewing point across the water towards Caernarfon castle and Snowdonia. That is the location for this painting. At low tide the strait is muddy and provides an ideal feeding ground for gulls and waders. The water lies in shallow pools and inlets, interrupted by breakwaters.
Muddy colours in a watercolour are undesirable but applied cleanly and with purpose the overall effect can be atmospheric.

The Wind Pump: Lanzarote 14 x 10¼ in
England is said to be the original home of watercolour because of the effects of the climate on the landscape and where conditions are often right for water to run off paper, or at least spread in a reasonably controlled manner, before eventually drying. Hence the soft edges which can be achieved.

When painting outdoors in arid conditions like those in the Canary Islands (not far from the Sahara desert) watercolour behaves quite differently, even if the paper is wetted beforehand. The light which comes back off the easel is also incredibly strong.

The Lanzarote coast-line is dotted with neglected wind pumps once used to lift sea water into shallow pans, the sun then evaporating it to salt. The hessian on many of the sails, stretched over a timber frame, suggests that not many would work today. Tourism is providing the income instead. I did my best with the dry conditions although my painting suggests that it will get thoroughly soaked if I don't soon run for cover!

Fishermen's Cottages 10 x 7 in
I cannot remember where the idea for this painting came from but it was obviously a day when I felt like painting something different.

It is best to think through the planning of a painting before applying the first colours. The sky is often the lightest part but it is revealing to discover what happens when tones are reversed (see also pp.90 & 125).

The need for some relief from the overall gloom had been anticipated by applying masking medium to high-light doors, windows, flowers and gable ends of the cottages nearest the sea. The masked areas were later touched in with bright, light tones, to bring the painting to life. Overall, the effect suggests an early lighting up time with quite a lot of rain and wind to come. It is an example of asking "what will happen if ..." I think it is a successful painting and proof that if you do not take risks with watercolour you will not learn the limits of the medium.

△ **Caernarfon Harbour** 18¾ x 13 in
Caernarfon is a market town and port at the entrance to the Menai Strait. The castle, once an early Roman station, is well-preserved; a robust structure remembered for the investiture of Prince Charles in 1969.

At Caernarfon you either paint the castle or the harbour. The scene is too broad to do justice to both in one painting. I decided on the harbour. On a sunny Sunday afternoon it was bustling with small craft which get in and out to sea through a horizontally pivoted bridge. My painting shows this colourful assortment of small boats against the background of port buildings and town houses.

▷ **Mid-Pacific: Fiji** 14 x 9¾ in
I had the opportunity to spend a weekend in
Suva on a business trip and with paints available
produced two watercolours (right and opposite).
This very simple painting, done briefly in front of
the subject, epitomises the ocean at Suva. It is a
dramatic slatey blue and reflects the fast changing
weather conditions around this island. The small
boat emphasises the loneliness of a vast ocean.
This seascape is painted with paynes grey which I
now assiduously avoid. It contains a very
powerful pigment and once on the palette
muddies all others. It may have some unique
uses, as here, but I now find myself better off
without it.
Lemon yellow is the only other colour in this
painting, just tinting the sky and the water to the
right of the sail.

◁ **Backwater: Caernarfon** 13¼ x 10 in
How different this painting is from the one
above; full of strong colour and sharp contrasts.
The corrugated iron shed and blue boat are
deliberately counter-changed against the
background. The tree shadows provide a touch of
mystery to the water and help establish the bright
reflections which give vitality to the painting.
Altogether this is a busy composition full of light
and interest, incorporating a wide palette of
yellows, reds, blues and greens to complement
the vigorous treatment.

36

△ **Entrance to Suva Harbour: Fiji**
13½ x 10 in
Early in the morning, before the sun was up,
I sat on a parapet overlooking Suva Bay,
knowing that within an hour it would be too
hot and sticky to paint and all the colours
would have changed. I arranged my paints.
Time was of the essence. I had to get the
subject down on paper quickly. Just a minute
or so of penciling in was enough.
I decided to keep the palette simple; paynes
grey again (see p.36), lemon yellow and
burnt umber. There may also have been a
touch of light red. I masked out the cruise
ship coming from the left and the white
building on the right.
The sky went in very quickly but took ages to
dry. I had to wait. The painting needed the
hard edges of the distant mountains and the
darker range in front. I had not the benefit of
a portable hair dryer to speed things up.
Finally I put in the promontory, the trees and
small boats, not wanting to over-complicate
it with too much detail.
Some watercolours benefit from working
under pressure and not having the
advantage of an easel or the studio to lay in
the washes. This is one of them. It has to
stand on its own merits.

△ **Evening: Lyme Regis** 10¾ x 8 in
The third painting of Lyme Regis in this Section is
very different from the others on pp.29 & 31. I
wanted to record the calm atmosphere of this
evening scene: the bathers have gone, the boats
have been moored and most tourists have left for
their hotels.
The low sun is just catching the sides of the
buildings. It is reflecting off the beach and highlighting part of the cob. The white masts were
carefully registered with masking medium and a
ruling pen before painting began.
The sun is also catching the undersides of the
clouds making quite an active sky. I have
therefore kept the sea quiet, painting it in simple
flat washes and resisting the temptation to
include people and boats, which I considered
distractions.
The palette consists of three main colours;
ultramarine, burnt sienna and raw sienna. These
are supported by small touches of cobalt blue in
the sea and sky and limited additions of
cadmium red to warm the buildings and cloud
shadows.

Towns & Villages

Some subjects need very little drawing before starting to paint. A landscape, for example, with perhaps distant trees and a couple of buildings can be sketched in a few minutes, to ensure that the horizon is appropriately placed and the principal subject well located. Minimal pencil work has the advantage that one is not tied too rigidly when starting to paint; the application of colour washes becomes a lot looser and therefore usually of better quality. Too much pencil work has the disadvantage that it often leads to too much rubbing out, in striving to be over-precise. Even a putty rubber can roughen the surface of the paper which, to my way of thinking, is sacrosanct.

When painting buildings in a village scene the perspective of roofs, eaves, chimneys and other architectural features has to be right, and time laying in the design is often very well spent. No amount of good colour work can correct an obvious fault in, perhaps, the proportions of windows and doorways, or their relationship, for example, to the height of people in the street. A rough drawing on a scrap of paper is an obvious help in becoming familiar with the subject; or a watercolour sketch in front of the subject, with all its faults, is a good basis for providing a more considered painting in the studio when the faults of the original can be fully understood and eliminated.

The word perspective often strikes fear into those new to painting. The painter's objective is to put the three-dimensional village scene now in front of him on to a two-dimensional surface, the paper. Achieving perspective in the painting means correctly portraying angles, such as roofs and eaves rising or sloping away, and the spacing of vertical dimensions, such as walls and doorways, as they recede into the distance.

I find that holding a piece of card up to the subject tells me a lot about these angles especially when it is difficult to judge whether a roof is rising or sloping away. The corner of the card can tell me whether the angle of a roof ridge at a gable end is just a little or a lot less than ninety degrees.

Eventually, with experience, drawing this type of scene in good perspective is no longer a problem.

It is simply a question of doing it often enough. Then the eye eventually and automatically establishes reference points during the drawing process against which other features are placed.

To paint a busy urban scene in front of the subject is often quite impossible and has to be done from rough sketches or photographs. I see no problem with this. Photographing a complex subject is a very helpful way of converting the three-dimensional scene into a two-dimensional image.

The other requirement when painting buildings is to get the smaller architectural details right such as the way in which a chimney stack sits on a roof, or windows are recessed into a wall and not stuck as appendages on the outside. Look carefully at the return under a soffit board and where the brackets go to hold a rain water down pipe. Drawing these small features a few times, quite separately from producing a painting, provides confidence for the next occasion. There is no doubt that those with "do it yourself" experience of building construction are at a distinct advantage when it comes to understanding and drawing architectural features.

The Church of St. Lorenzo: Florence
14½ x 10¼ in
Many photographs record my visits to Florence, of the buildings and streets as material for paintings. Here the church of St. Lorenzo provides an impressive backcloth to the people at the market stalls.

The roofs and arches provide a very strong perspective. They direct attention to the red domes and lanterns, strong Italian sunlight draining the colour from these huge cupolas. I have put in quite a lot of architectural detail in the warm stones and blue shadows for which Florence is renowned.

Hillside Village: Elba 12 x 8¼ in
The village in this painting is perched precariously high up on the hill side. The buildings and trees hug the contours. The church tower stands proud against the sky. The strong diagonal in this L-shaped composition fixes the subject and gives it stability.

Riding into Cowden 19¾ x 13¼ in
Horse riding is very popular in this area with riding schools nearby. Horses in the lanes and villages are very much in keeping with our local countryside. The two riders in the painting are in Cowden, just a few miles up the road from our gallery.

Bird in Hand Street – Groombridge 18 x 12 in
The old part of Groombridge sits astride the Kent/Sussex border, about four miles from Tunbridge Wells. My wife and I lived there for twenty years.

A lot of new housing has been built, but the village green, with its older 17th century properties of brick, tile and weather-boarding remain. Little has changed on the green. Many of the houses were once shops and their names are still there to remind us of what was sold.

Bird-in-Hand Street, just wide enough for two cars to pass, is on the left of the village green and winds up towards Burrswood (p.151). To the right is The Crown (see opposite), a well-frequented pub. The green is usually dotted with people at weekends enjoying a drink in the summer sun.

P.B. CORNWELL

40

▽ **Groombridge Hill** 20½ x 13¼ in

Groombridge Hill leads down to The Crown on the village green (see opposite). My painting is of the back of the pub, between large oaks, casting useful four o'clock shadows across the road. These direct the eye to the middle distance of the painting where the complex roof shapes jutting in different directions, some in light, others in shadow, are painted in warm tones.

The way to the pub is further emphasised by the post and rail fencing (right) and chestnut fencing (left). The light on the meadow also makes a contribution.

A lot of colour mixes are used in the trees. The canopies are in shade but sufficient sky holes have been left to keep the branch structure open. There is a small group of people waiting outside the pub for a bus into Tunbridge Wells. It still provides a regular, if infrequent, service.

P.B.CORNWELL

The Pantiles from the Chalybeate Wells : Tunbridge Wells 19½ x 14 in

Royal Tunbridge Wells is a spa town with iron-rich springs discovered around 1600. "The Pantiles" is its oldest street, a colonnaded shopping arcade originally paved with baked tiles in the reign of Queen Anne. It is now surfaced with Purbeck flagstones. The Chalybeate Wells are at the north end of the Pantiles.

Such a well-known place has to be immediately recognisable in a painting, but the Pantiles is not an easy subject. The street is not flat but domed. The colonnade consists of columns with regular spacing and when seen from one end they recede in a precise manner. They are not all the same height and the buildings above have obviously different floor levels, evident from the variation in window sills and window heights.

In this painting and the one opposite the columns have been preserved as 'lights'. Only then could the shop doorways and windows be painted in shadow. Even so, some bright reflections had to be kept for the windows themselves.

Most of the mature hornbeams which characterised the Pantiles were uprooted in the 1987 storm and have been replaced by smaller specimens. I prefer to paint it as it was. Here and in the painting opposite I have tried to create a feeling of sunlight, largely by the discreet use of shadows.

The Pantiles from 'Binns': Tunbridge Wells
20¼ x 13¾ in

'Binns' is a long-established tea shop on the Pantiles catering especially for the many tourists who come to the town.

In this painting and the one opposite a lot of preliminary masking out was done to allow uninterrupted application of colour washes. For the windows and for some of the finer columns the fluid was applied by pen. Where there are people standing against darks, I preferred to mask them too. All this was done early in the painting process to avoid a lot of colour lifting and scratching out later.

Most of the sunlight in the painting is either white paper, or described by touches of lemon yellow and naples yellow. The street is raw sienna with very dilute additions of light red and cadmium orange. The hanging tiles and flagstones are barely hinted at. The shadows on the sunlit buildings and street are cobalt blue with slight additions of cadmium red. The trees are deliberately sombre to direct even more attention to the lighter parts of the painting, mostly in the centre.

△ **Rooms to Let: Aberdovey** 14½ x 10¼ in
Aberdovey is a small resort on the west coast of
Wales. The town is on the north side of an
estuary with wide sand banks at low tide.
Rooms to Let is one of three shop front
paintings in this Section. I like the canopies
over the Post Office and the reflected colour in
the windows. The pillar box is faithfully
represented, except for the black band around
the bottom which is ugly (and we all know why
that's there!).
The landlady of the holiday accommodation
brings life to the painting. Framing her in the
attractive doorway accentuates this figure.
She is obviously keen on keeping her hanging
baskets in good shape. The sign boards add
interesting detail.

44

The Post Office at Firle 14 x 10¼ in

Firle is a hamlet at the foot of the South Downs where the Post Office is the only shop. The windows are full of reflected colour. The small panes are characteristic of this age of property and I especially like the red pelmets.

It is June and the window boxes are in full bloom. The name over the door, the old wooden seat and the old fashioned post-box, in cadmium red, all add authenticity. The advertisement for the local newspaper is a sign of the times. In Firle there's time to talk. Hours pass quite slowly here. The two 'locals' are taking a few minutes from their not too busy day to discuss important events.

The entire painting is in one plane except for the low wall and small patch of sky, a repeat of the window format. The most difficult areas to paint were the flint facings, characteristic of walls and buildings in this part of the country. They require careful treatment. Flints reflect light and need to sparkle. They are best portrayed by painting just the irregular jointing. The bricks around the door and windows impart warmth and set off the green doorway.

Firle Stores
Prop RW Reece   Est. 1780

FIRLE POST OFFICE

EASTBOURNE
WORKERS
GET MORE
CLOUT

Lady Street from the Guildhall: Lavenham
12¾ x 9½ in

Lavenham is a Suffolk wool town, but sheep have been replaced by cereals. In August-September the town and surrounding villages are aware that it is harvest time. Heavy grain lorries are an unfortunate but necessary evil in late summer.

The town is full of original features. Buildings in the market square (p.52) and roads leading off, retain much of the character of the Middle Ages. This painting shows part of the Tudor Guildhall and the half-timbered houses leading down to the Swan Hotel. Lady Street is on a hill and the strongly sloping roofs lead down to where a couple of figures are walking up. Details of the buildings, their sagging roofs and often leaning chimneys need to be carefully drawn. The coloured renderings to the buildings in Suffolk make them interesting to paint. In this scene these strong colours and especially the 'negative shapes' between the trunks, branches and foliage of the trees keep the eye within the painting. I think it was these strong contrasts of shape and colour that encouraged me to paint it.

Welsh Village: Penally 9½ x 7 in
This scene was painted on a bright sunny afternoon. I was attracted by the variously shaped and coloured roofs, the old barn to the left and especially the church with its short square tower and triangular top.

There was almost no traffic so I stood with my easel at the side of the road for a couple of hours. The village nestles against a hillside of dark trees, helping to outline the much lighter buildings.

The lane leading into the painting was a 'gift', sufficiently to one side not to be too obvious. It makes you feel you would like to go to the end and explore what's there.

The foreground was laid in without detail, simple vertical brush strokes completing a quiet sunny atmosphere.

The Toll House: Chiddingly 11¼ x 7¼ in
I have painted this small group of buildings twice and on both occasions tried to squeeze drama out of the white walls and a loosely painted sky. The scene is lit by late afternoon sun. The long shadows on the road and the light on the buildings give the subject depth. The sky was painted with very little care. The main branches of the trees were inserted while the paint of the foliage was still wet. Here, colour mixing was happening on the paper. Who was I to interfere with it. My only involvement was to slightly dampen the sky close to the foliage to defuse the edge. The chimney stacks, white gates and the sign post at the end of the road are small details which bring the painting to life. Turn right and within a few hundred yards you come to Chiddingly church (over the page).

△ **Autumn Colours: Chiddingly** 19½ x 12 in
Many photographs were used to decide how
best to paint this subject with a light steeple
caught by the sun against a darker sky. The
area in front of the church is a cricket ground,
but it is better if left textured and unkempt,
the small pavilion omitted and the imaginary
post and rail fence introduced.

When using photographs to help plan a
painting and remind me of a subject I find it
best to disregard colours and plan my own
palette. I also find that if I paint quickly things
go well, and masking out allows me to do that.
I can then spend time after removing the
masking medium getting the finer details of
the buildings right.

The Old Post Office: Penshurst 20 x 14 in

A covered archway leads to Penshurst church and this cherry tree is at the entrance. For most of the year it looks quite dreary but come Spring when it is fully out and the ground littered with blossom, it is delightful.

The softness of the tree has been set against the harder lines of the buildings. That on the left provides an important dividing line in the painting and must appear to come forward. The cherry blossoms, the fence and window were first masked out and the cherry tree painted with a lot of softened edges. If this could not be achieved easily and convincingly there would be no point in taking the painting further. Satisfied with the result I then painted the chimney and roofs around it, again keeping most edges soft. The detail in the fence, the litter bin and the window is essential to the centre of the painting. The rest is painted quite casually and I am very happy with the result. I especially like the blossom and the light catching parts of the fence.

△ **The Village Stores** 13¼ x 9½ in
Bay windows are not easy to paint. All the
panes are of course the same size but must be
drawn gradually reducing in width to the sides.
Generally the inside of a shop is dark but items
in the window are illuminated from outside.
These lights interact with reflected light from
the glass itself. All this may seem common
sense, but now come to paint it!
The Village Stores with its hanging baskets and
flowers around the open door is entirely
imaginary. It comes from looking at many
similar shops, for example in Lavenham. The
overall blue in the painting is reflected sky. The
figure in the door gives human interest and
invites you in.

50

Sally Lunn's Tea Shop: Bath 14 x 10¼ in
This well-known tea shop gets its name from a
sweet spongy tea-cake sold by a girl in the streets
of Bath some 200 years ago. You can now eat
them inside but it is invariably crowded.
Bath has a natural charm. The attractive bay
window of this building and the intricately
designed leaded-light over the door are all part of
it. The upper floor is faced with yellow bath stone
and bears a blue plaque which identifies the
building.
This subject makes a good painting not only
because of the interesting windows and signs, but
also because of the wrought iron work to the left
which I believe surrounds a Branch of National
Westminster Bank.
The people looking into the shop are seen from
the inside in the next painting.

Tea at Sally Lunn's 13½ x 10¼ in
This painting is based on a photograph. The
family looking in at the window are taking a
long time to make up their minds whether to
come in or not, whilst the couple of elderly
ladies already having tea are enjoying every
bit of it. The window is filled with baskets of
bread and confectionery. The red curtains
above and on a rail across the window
provide customers with some privacy.
I like the light on the table cloth and the
china, and especially the reflections from the
lady's spectacles. Both ladies seem very
engrossed in their tea and conversation. I
wonder what the local gossip is today?

51

△ **Market Square: Lavenham** 19¼ x 12½ in
The wide market square at Lavenham was laid out in the 13th century. It is surrounded by Tudor houses and the well-preserved Guildhall. A 20th century 'Hovis' sign hangs over the bakery. The shop next door sells everything you need for a good packed lunch.

It is late in the afternoon and the sun is just managing to get over the sagging roofs and light the buildings opposite, casting long diagonal shadows. The morning rain still lies in puddles. At this time of day most of the people in the square are tourists, perhaps come to visit the little antique shop on the corner. The cross in the centre of the square dates back to 1501 and provides a convenient place to sit and admire the buildings.

Ultramarine, light red and a little burnt sienna were used to paint the roofs. I modified the mixes to get variety, with the lightest tones on the buildings further away. I used raw sienna for the street and the cross. Cobalt blue in the sky was repeated in the puddles.

△ **The Village Pump : Castle Coombe** 14 x 10¼ in
Castle Coombe, in Wiltshire, is widely known as
the "prettiest village in England" from the award
won in 1962. It was once a cloth weaving centre.
The attractive cottages are 15th century and built
of local Cotswold stone.

In the centre of the village is a covered market
cross which was once used for selling wool. Here
is a corner of that building, one of the pillars
supporting the roof. The very weathered stone is
portrayed by carefully modelling the shadows
where erosion has occurred.

But the principal subject of the composition is
the close up of the cast iron pump and the stone
sink of flowers. These have been treated as an
outdoor still life using strong colours to create
three dimensions.

Behind the pump is a soft tonal rendering of the
stone cottages which make Castle Coombe so
attractive to visitors.

▷ **Penshurst from the Meadows** 19 x 12¾ in
The church at Penshurst with its easily recognised
pinnacles is originally 13th century but with considerable reconstruction. It stands above a group
of 19th century half-timbered cottages. The best
view is from the meadow alongside the river
Medway. You then look up to the tower and an
assortment of cottage roofs and chimneys against
the sky. The buildings are fortunately softened by
mature trees which are used in this painting to
break hard lines and give the impression that the
subject is well-settled into the landscape.
A lot of preparatory drawing is needed to get the
perspectives right. The angled roofs, gable ends,
one building overlapping another, the chimneys
of different heights, windows and shadows, have
got to be thought about before painting begins.
Then this considerable detail must be balanced
by quiet, uncluttered areas in the painting the sky
and foreground landscape. The small fence on
the right gives a useful lead in to this panorama.

▽ **Wash Day** 8½ x 6¼ in
How well a dark sky emphasises sunlight in a
painting! The trees put the church and adjacent
cottages into strong relief. The empty foreground
emphasises all that is going on behind.
This is a small village near Machynlleth in West
Wales. The gable ends of the buildings, jutting in
different directions, provide strong patterns of
light and shade. The gates, washing line and two
women chatting are deliberately painted against
dark backgrounds. There is a wind blowing; a
good drying day.

△ **Old Houses: Cowden** 11½ x 9¼ in
Cowden is about 3 miles from our studio. The
blacksmiths, the school, post office and shop
have gone. So too has one of the pubs. It is a
small village of just a few houses, tile-hung and
weather-boarded, looked over by the high church
steeple.
Paintings of local interest are always welcome in
exhibitions. Parris House (originally 'Parish') with
its long sloping roofs is typical of Cowden. The
tree casts loosely painted shadows against white
walls and the shadows on the road and distant
cottages help emphasise sunlight. Scale in the
painting is provided by the group of people
standing outside the old dairy.

△ **Blue Shutters : Beddgelert** 12 x 8¾ in
"Surroundings of awe-inspiring beauty make
Beddgelert one of the most memorable villages
in Britain" *(quote: AA Book of British Villages)*.
It nestles within the landscape of the Snowden
range. There is much to paint here, the
mountains, the bridges over the river Glaslyn, or
this group of cottages on the village green.
I am always looking for small architectural details
which are a challenge to paint and lend
authenticity. Here it is the blue shutters on the
central cottage, some windows open, others
closed, the arched porches and the small white
railings on the low brick wall.
The long roof would be uninteresting but for the
central chimney and the light on the mountains
behind. The tree in the foreground frames the
buildings and pushes them back into the middle
distance. Notice how the shadows on the ground
identify the raised pathway.

The Almond Tree 14 x 10½ in

About 40 years ago I saw an almond tree in bloom, its pink flowers on otherwise bare, charcoal-coloured branches, against bright red bricks of a municipal building. It was February. All else in that wet main street was grey. The scene made a lasting impression.

Many years later, *The Almond Tree* was painted using a backcloth of Oxford buildings; warm stonework painted with washes of yellow ochre and mixes of cadmium red and neutral tint.

The tree occupies prime position in the painting. The outline is loose and shows the rather twisted trunk and branches. Small spots of masking medium pick out the blossoms, touched in later with very dilute colour.

The area of light in the background draws the viewer right through to the small groups of people in silhouette. The buildings contain just enough detail to identify the main features. This painting provided the experience for *The Old Post Office : Penshurst* (p.49).

P.B. CORNWELL

Cathedral of the Downs 20½ x 13½ in
The 14th century church at Alfriston with stonework of small cut flints sits by the river Cuckmere. There is a further painting of it on p.(100) and a painting of the nearby Clergy House on p.(59). Alfriston village, of medieval origins, lies within the chalk Downs about three miles from the sea.

The trees on the left of the painting and the broken outline of the Downs form a diagonal line towards the church with its well-described window of the north transept. The two conifers repeat the shape of the short spire. The bare tree and light coloured shrubbery soften the outline of the church, the whole giving a verdant, almost luxuriant atmosphere.

P.B. CORNWELL

◁ **October Morning: Lower Slaughter** 12 x 8½ in
A Cotswold painting with very little definition to create the softness of a misty morning. The muted colours, raw sienna and umbers, have a very narrow tonal range except for the tree trunk and reflections in the water. A very different painting from that of Alfriston church (opposite). All the shapes in the foreground reinforce the curve of the river. The small white bridge acts as a stop. The river turns towards the base of the tree and to the couple walking their dog. The almost imperceptible cadmium red on the man's coat provides the only spot of brightness.
The convincing autumnal atmosphere is very pleasing. It required a lot of local wetting of the paper as the washes were applied.

▷ **The Clergy House: Alfriston** 9½ x 6¾ in
The Clergy House, which was the first building to come under care of the National Trust, is just a short step from Alfriston church (opposite). This low white building backing on to the river gets immediate attention against a sombre background of the Downs.
The small white gate by the cottage, pieces of broken fencing, and the river banks of horizontal washes give variety of texture and shape to the foreground.

△ **Bend in the Road** 13½ x 10¼ in
A sunny day late in the year, a strong wind
blowing and atmosphere provided by fleeting
clouds. Extensive use of cobalt blue describes a
chilly scene, but winter sunshine provides a lot of
brightness and interesting shadow patterns across
the road.
This is Derbyshire. The cottages are gaunt. The
stone walls around the fields have had little
repair. The opening into the field has lost its gate
and the tree has suffered storm damage. It is a
vigorous painting with the oil drum providing a
strong spot of colour.

The Maltings near Clare 14½ x 10¼ in
Clare is a small village on the river Stour. The
square wooden grille on the top of the maltings
is a common feature throughout Suffolk.
Many tonal changes identify the succession of
building against tree and one tree against another
to make a pattern of interesting shapes, using
hard lines against soft and vice versa. The simple
sky and foreground are restful areas to escape
into but the little ditch and bridge have vitality.
Brick and Flint (also on this page) was painted
on the same day.

Brick and Flint 13¾ x 9¾ in
Another building with a roof feature and
small dormer windows, but I am not sure
what it is used for. I stood at my easel for a
couple of hours but no one came or went. It
is probably a school during vacation.
There are two strong contrasts in this
painting. The brick of the house against the
flint wall and the dark upright conifers
contrasted with the loosely painted ash trees.
I like their light slender trunks and the
foliage blending into the sky.
The high flint wall and the lower fencing on
the right seem to lock the building in their
grip, imparting stability to the composition.

◁ **Passing the Time of Day: Aldborough** 12 x 9 in
What attracted me to this subject was the pattern of light on the trees and the way the trunks and branches hid parts of the buildings, leaving much to be imagined. There is a lot of warm colour and textured surfaces; the roofs, the walls, the open door and the roadway.
The two women chatting are important to the overall atmosphere and are so placed to help the perspective and depth in the painting.

▷ **Cottages near Walsingham** 9 x 6¾ in
The two villages of Little and Great Walsingham are in a very rural part of Norfolk, just south of Wells-next-the-Sea.
I parked by the edge of the road and set up my easel on the leeward side. There was quite a breeze blowing. A rough pencil sketch took only a few moments, placing the buildings and outlining the trees. The road ahead was straight. I decided to give it a slight curve.
The dark trees on the left emphasise the white gable end. The chimney pots, roofs and trees make a strong boundary between the landscape and the sky. The arrangement of the cottages, sideways and end on, give this sky line variety. It is this irregular but pleasing line which attracted me to this subject in the first place. The rest of the painting, the fields and hedgerows provide a simple support for the cottages on the hill. The scenery is typical of the inland countryside of Norfolk.

Trees & Woodlands

I have been interested in drawing and painting trees for as long as I can remember. I am not quite sure why they have become a favourite subject, since describing their form and pattern of growth is no less important than setting down correctly the architecture and perspective of a row of houses. Perhaps the interest came when I was quite young from learning to recognise the commoner species from my grandfather when he took my brother and me, as evacuees, for long walks in the Hertfordshire countryside. I began to take pride in recognising the different species from their leaves, bark and their way of growing. This was at a time when many children from the cities, at an impressionable age, saw the countryside for the first time.

This interest in trees was further added to when, during the 1940's, I took part in school forestry camps to clear fell areas of woodland in southern England for pit props and cord wood, as a contribution towards the war effort. I can think of no better way of coming to terms with trees than, as a teenager, being given an axe for a month and progressively felling, cutting and burning through acres of woodland. That was before the word "environment" became part of common speech.

My interest in trees was further advanced by studying tropical agriculture in Trinidad and Guyana. There, over the course of a year, I was introduced to the "economic" trees; banana, oil

△ **Shade on the Path** 8¼ x 6¼ in
A small painting in which the slope of the land contributes to the design, sweeping down to the path which then turns gently away. The fence and tree trunks put the interest in the centre of the painting. The tree to the right provides needed variation in colour which places it a little further back.

palm, coconut, rubber, cocoa, citrus and many others. I also had the opportunity to see trees like mangrove growing naturally in the swamps edging the great rivers in Guyana.

But perhaps my closest relationship with trees and my strongest liking for them came from working over four years in the tropical rain forests of West Africa. Here were the real giants of enormous girth, with buttress roots as high as a house spreading many feet from the bottom of the trunk. But they were still not wide enough to stop the silk cotton trees from blowing over in a tropical storm, each bringing down others, like so many match sticks, in an area the size of a football pitch.

More recently I have been planting a lot of different species at Bassetts Mill; beech, birch, oak, larch and ornamentals, especially the early flowering cherries which make the spring come early on warm winter days.

The hurricane of September 1987 did an important job in destroying large numbers of trees in the south of England, stimulating regeneration from damaged branches and encouraging great areas of replanting. That storm stimulated an awareness of the importance of trees in the landscape, especially when people were advised that some 10 million trees had been lost overnight.

Drawing and painting trees, especially in woodland, is initially quite a challenge, and not being able to see the wood for the trees is never more true. But success eventually comes from learning to be selective, composing the painting, incorporating quite strong lighting to emphasise form, making trunks appear three-dimensional and using branch shadows across the trunks and adjacent branches to emphasise roundness.

Branches arise from the trunk in quite an orderly way, at angles which are almost constant for any particular species. They do not usually taper towards the end but reduce step by step at each point from which smaller branches arise. The level at which branches grow out from the trunk and the angle of slope relative to the ground are all details which must be recognised to make the subject appear convincing.

Above all, except perhaps in mid-summer, you can invariably see branches and sky through the leaf canopies of trees. This makes them look much less heavy when painted.

▷ **Oak Trees: Suffolk** 10 x 7½ in
Strong perspective and bright sunlight make this a good subject. On this sort of day shade would have been welcome to reduce the fierce light reflecting off the paper.
My view is across open ground with small ditches either side of the track. Detail is kept for the trees, especially the lower branches where side-lighting models the blue-grey trunks and gives long shadows over the warm ploughed field.

△ **Dappled Shade** 20¼ x 13¾ in
These beech trees are in our garden, but unfortunately the big one at the top was lost in the 1987 storm.

The pale background was washed in first leaving just a small patch of sky. The colours in the foliage were repeated in the trunks and care taken to leave spaces to let the sunlight through. I made a special effort to place dark edges of trunks against light background to ensure depth to the painting. The slope up to the right was helpful in putting the two groups of trees on separate levels. The distant light trunks were held back with masking medium.

I like the central patch of sunlight which encourages the viewer to walk through the woodland, and the small dark branches growing downward on the left, a detail characteristic of beeches. They will often root.

A lot of different colour mixes were used in the foreground, burnt sienna, raw umber, raw sienna, with prussian blue and ultramarine to give a range of warm browns and greens.

Sussex Beeches (I & II) 20 x 12½ in and 20 x 12¼ in

These paintings, below and opposite, are a pair. They were produced in the studio from sketches and experience of drawing trees. In both, a principal foreground tree is set against a background of minor players which takes the viewer through the painting and keeps him within the picture frame.

The warm grey woodland in *Sussex Beeches I* provides a soft background. The trunks and foliage of the foreground tree give a particularly solid and robust feel to it. The smaller tree sloping in on the extreme left not only defines the edge of the painting but repeats the diagonal line of the foreground tree.

The thicket of trees in the distance of *Sussex Beeches II* (opposite) is somewhat threatening, but helps to strengthen the sunlit foreground. In both paintings I have used cadmium yellow pale for much of the ground work and yellow ochre for sunlit foliage. The background colours were of course put in first, working forward as the paintings progressed.

P.B.CORNWELL

66

Ashdown: Sunday Morning 19½ x 13¼ in
What a very strong sense of scale the people give
to this painting! I have varied their heights to give
the impression of a happy family outing. They
provide a balance with the large foreground tree.
The hazy sky and distant trees were laid in first
leaving a small area of light for the walkers. The
main tree is a beech with spreading roots, many
above the ground. The intricate pattern of light
and dark branches is the result of low sunlight.
The pattern is repeated in the more distant trees
and gives an overall impression of a clear bright
winter's day.

△ **Autumn Symphony** 14 x 10¼ in
Woodland affords many subjects for autumn and
winter paintings. Here trunks and branches are
described against darker washes of cobalt blue
and cadmium red. Beeches are strong subjects
and with plenty of sunlight show their form.
The strong earth line which separates the
background is placed almost half way up the
picture frame. Below it is a generous description
of the slope with flowing branch shadows. The
upper part of the painting is divided by the large
trunks into three smaller rectangles with
descriptive light and dark patterns.
Autumn Symphony has a lot of movement, with
the branches of one tree crossing in front of
another and the exposed roots and buttressed
trunks providing orchestrated shapes.

Birches and Bracken 20½ x 13½ in
I took many photographs in this piece of woodland to get material for a painting, this thicket of birches and bracken. I used black and white to get correct tonal values.

There is no opaque colour (guache). All the highlights, the twisted fronds and finer branches, were carefully masked out first. This required some tedious drawing, the whole sheet of paper held back where I wanted lights. It took a long time, and of course not until later did I know whether all this preparatory work had been successful.

Strong tones went into the sky with rich purple for the background trees, so typical of birches in winter. The white areas were touched in with yellow ochre, raw sienna and lemon yellow. Hard edges were softened where masking medium was removed. Small areas in the bracken requiring better definition were meticulously darkened. This was a high-risk painting which could so easily have gone wrong. Some courage and anticipation were needed during the initial planning. Masking out was essential to achieve the loose washes of pure watercolour for this subject.

October Trees 14¼ x 10¼ in
Here is an opportunity to use 'hot' mixes of cadmium yellow pale, burnt sienna with touches of light red and cadmium orange. These have been contrasted with strong blue-greens mixed from prussian blue. The tree trunks are patterned with warm greys and sombre greens.

The foreground is laid in very simply to compliment the vigorous description of the branches. Light catches the turn in the road. A strong painting with invigorating colour.

Autumn: Groombridge 13 x 10 in
Coming down through Groombridge, sight of this magnificent oak provides striking autumn colour year after year. I have used mixes of prussian blue to provide the darks in the foliage with slightly stronger washes for the branches. The white house across the road, aptly named Oak Cottage, with the skyline of roofs and chimneys provides depth and balance in the painting.

Springtime on Ashdown 20¾ x 14 in
A silent, peaceful and undisturbed afternoon is the essence of this painting. Two paths converge in the centre leading the viewer into the sunlight. The sun also penetrates the foliage to give loose patches of colour.
The feeling of spring is created by soft greens and yellows. The foreground trees set the distance apart. Shade contrasts with the open sunny area which beckons to be explored. White stitchwort sparkles among dark shadows in the foreground. The grassy banks were added very loosely to describe uneven ground.

72

Against the Light 20 x 14 in
I wanted to create the impression of a break in the woodland with light coming through a clearing. Full brush loads of colour with the pigments inter-mixing on the paper were used to record this scene. Working from the back to the front I was not sure whether enough strengths had been left for the foreground. The colour had to be applied quickly and intensely always keeping it transparent.

First the hazy background was painted with cobalt blue. Then the sunlight of pure lemon yellow, allowing it to mix on the paper. The ridge across the painting describes the limit of the foreground and had to be kept light. Next the trees were added making them warmer in the foreground. Finally the shadows coming towards me. These had to be put in once and cleanly with very dark tones, keeping some edges soft and others hard.

P.B.CORNWELL.

△ **Sunshine and Shadow** 20½ x 14 in
Not many trees stand upright. Not many trees
have brown trunks and with beeches a smooth
grey-green is common, often tending towards
pale blue. The texture is also characteristic;
almost a satin feel to the bark with very few
surface irregularities unless the beeches are
very old. These observations come together in
this painting. Beeches hold their branches
almost like the roof on a house, sometimes
layering gently downwards. Overall they create a
majestic impression, firmly planted in the ground
with strong buttressed roots. High leaf fall and
light exclusion discourage growth beneath.

74

△ **Birches on Ashdown** 20 x 13¼ in
Birches are no less attractive (see "Beeches" opposite) but they grow like weeds, quickly colonising bare patches and finding the most inhospitable places to survive. They twist this way and that, appearing to compete for light with many trunks arising from the same base. They favour sandy locations among gorse and pines and Ashdown is a good example.

I painted this group on a small mound because of the exposed roots, and of course the silvered bark. Their finer branches are almost needle thin and in winter create a bluish purple haze as in the background here.

P.B. CORNWELL.

△ **Sussex Snowfall** 20¾ x 13¾ in
A winter scene with snow, driven by the wind,
clinging to the sides of trees. See how the overall
whiteness of the scene emphasises the darks at
this cold uninviting time. The weak sun provides
a glimmer of warmth in tones of raw sienna and
burnt umber. There is a lot more snow to come
in the sky.

◁ **Out for a Walk: Suffolk** 10¾ x 6¾ in
Suffolk is known for its low horizons and big skies. Large blocks of trees are common; gently rounded shapes which punctuate large expanses of cultivated land.

A simple graded wash served for the sky and warm mixes of cobalt blue and yellow ochre for the distant trees. There is a couple walking in the lane. They emphasise the quiet open countryside.

▽ **Pines near King's Standing: Ashdown** 14 x 10 in
Ashdown is only a few miles from our gallery. It was once well-wooded but became progressively felled for smelting. It is common land now used for recreation and sheep grazing. Herds of deer can sometimes be seen in the early morning.

I have tried to capture the growth of pine trees, their outline, the branches and tufts of needles turning up towards the sky. Young pines provide dense shade and a mosaic of filtered light on the trunks.

On the far side of the path are clumps of gorse which in hot dry summers create a fire risk. In the foreground I have used mixes of cobalt blue and cadmium red to represent the extensive heathers.

Beeches 21 x 14¼ in

This painting is based on pencil sketches of individual trees. I then grouped them to make a satisfying composition, choosing an unusual viewpoint looking slightly downwards.

A sunlit trace separates the shadows of the beeches from the open woodland beyond. The shaded area is cool. I used a silvery blue for the trees (cobalt) with varied warmer ground colours here and there, where the sun manages to get through. A single dark yew tree provides good contrast.

78

The Medway at Fordcombe

The river Medway rises not far from Forest Row and forms the Kent-Sussex boundary for many miles. The lake in our garden eventually runs into it about a mile or so before it reaches Fordcombe. Here are the upper reaches of what becomes a large river many miles away at Rochester, where it joins the Thames.

At Fordcombe the Medway is no more than a few metres wide, depending on the season (see p.81). It provides many opportunities for painting pastoral scenes and as it is only a couple of miles from our gallery, paintings of the river are now almost expected at exhibitions.

Here is the atmosphere of lazy afternoons, people fishing, cows in the meadows and time passing very slowly. It is best captured in half-imperial paintings which are able to convey that calm and tranquillity. Anything smaller and the painting can tend to become a little tight. The banks are wooded in places and the mixture of shadows and reflections from an unruffled surface are an essential part of the scene. Just half a dozen colours suffice.

However, all this calm is shattered at least once a year by the Ashurst to Fordcombe raft race, where craft of little more than a few planks tied to a couple of oil drums are launched into the river. I have not tried to paint this event.

△ **The Bridge at Fordcombe** 13¼ x 9½ in
The iron bridge at Fordcombe is one of many subjects I have painted near our gallery. To the left are the *Cottages by the Medway : Fordcombe* (p.80) and to the right *Fordcombe Meadows* (p.138). *The Willows at Fordcombe* (p.85) was also painted here. The area is low lying and often flooded.

The painting is very much understated, quite unpretentious, but a faithful record of this little bit of the village on the way to Tunbridge Wells.

Cottages by the Medway: Fordcombe

20½ x 13¾ in

The cottages at Fordcombe sit above the river overlooking a bank of wild flowers. Evening primrose, foxgloves, policeman's helmet and ragwort all grow here. In the spring it is white with the flowers of blackthorn. The bank drops down sharply to the water's edge where swans occasionally rest. It is an idyllic scene with farmland beyond.

These cottages are a favourite subject for painting, especially in bright sunlight with strong reflections in the water. The nearby trees accentuate these reflections to make this an attractive watercolour of vibrant light and shade.

△ **The Medway at Fordcombe** 19 x 12½ in
The river at Fordcombe flows through a wide
valley. Most of the year it reflects a mirror image
of willows but occasionally it turns into a torrent
of floodwater (see over).

In summer this is a lazy pastoral scene with
cows or sheep in the fields and a few people
fishing from the bank.
I pass here two or three times a week. I invariably
slow down. The view is never the same.

Winter Flood: Fordcombe 20¼ x 13 in
One November morning when the Medway was in flood I made a mental impression of the scene. To paint it would need only a few colours, mainly cerulean blue, raw sienna and burnt sienna. It was a chilly day but the clouds were well broken and there were still some autumn colours in the fields.

Back in my studio I got to work immediately. The trees were still holding on to a few leaves but had to be painted loosely against the sky. There were lights on the flood water and the tree trunks were in dark shadow.
The painting was completed in a couple of hours, full of clear washes and strong colour.

82

△ **Bridge over Kent Water** 19¾ x 13¾ in
This attractive bridge with its post and rail fence
could be passed almost unnoticed in its tangle of
undergrowth.
There is a lot of distance in this painting from the
close up of the bricks to the oast house beyond,
framed by the tree. There are also lots of
contrasts, from the strong darks under the bridge
and in the cool dark foliage, to the lightly painted
fields.
In recent years flax has been grown here
providing a sea of pale blue, a much lighter tone
than the sky, especially when the sun opens the
flowers for a brief period at mid-day.

△ **Cattle Grazing at Fordcombe** 21 x 13¾ in
From the way these cows have their noses
pressed against the fence it is obviously greener
on the other side.

Here is a lazy summer afternoon with just a few
clouds and light reflecting off the fields, warm
foreground trees and cooler woodland behind.

The river is painted with strong shadows,
reflections and surface vegetation.

Altogether this is a quiet rural scene, except for
the electricity pole which has an important job in
this s-shaped composition, marked out by the
river bank, the fence and cows and the edge of
the woodland.

Willows at Fordcombe 20¼ x 12¾ in

This is the last of the Fordcombe river scenes. It captures the atmosphere along the bank, the texture of the overhanging trees and their reflections in the water.

The darker trees on the left bank act as a foil for the blue-grey foliage of the willows, painted in cool washes of cobalt blue and yellow ochre. The paint was applied as blotches of colour with detail confined to a few small twigs along the bottom edge. I kept the willows in light tones to convey their loose open structure. The fields were laid in with warm tones of yellow ochre and small patches of lemon yellow.

The painting gives an overall impression of a quiet summer's day with not even the sound of water breaking the silence.

Pin Mill

The Suffolk coast for some thirty miles north of the Stour and Orwell estuaries is a wilderness of marshes and mud flats, one of the least spoilt areas of England. At the mouths of these two rivers are the industrial ports of Harwich and Felixstowe, but inland are two wide tidal rivers with muddy banks; waterways which were once important trade routes to Maningtree and Ipswich. Suffolk's network of streams drain its heavy clay cornfields through these large rivers to the sea.

Pin Mill is on the south bank of the Orwell some ten miles inland. It is now primarily a boating centre with an active yacht club. Boats are still built and launched from the yard. But Pin Mill also has the remains of old Thames barges and the ambience of past days when river traffic moved goods by sail. There is evidence that centuries ago, Pin Mill had a salt pan for processing salt from sea water.

The paintings in this Section show Pin Mill as it is today. It is an ideal place for painting boats and muddy shore lines.

P.B.CORNWELL

◁ **Summer Morning: Pin Mill** 20 x 13¼ in
A bright breezy morning. The air is especially
clear and as usual the atmosphere in this painting
is keyed to the sky.
All my colours were prepared in advance so that I
could dip into the palette and apply them as
quickly as possible. By this means the washes
remained clean. There was no time or need to go
back over what was already done. The colours
mixed themselves together gradually over the
paper's surface and time had to be allowed to let
this happen.

The clouds provide variety in the shadows
along the distant bank, strong enough to show
up the tiny boats in front. It is important to get
the finer details of boats and their rigging correct,
especially this sailing barge with sunlight on the
mast and furled sails.
The foreground was a delight to paint; so many
colours, including cadmium orange and cobalt
violet. Light reflected off pools of water was
interspersed with drier areas of different shades
of yellows and greens. A few people are standing
about enjoying this muddy river-side atmosphere.

△ **Barges on the Hard: Pin Mill** 20 x 14 in
'Messing about in boats' seems to be the
preoccupation of many who come to Pin Mill.
These parents with young children, however, are
happy to play around in muddy pools.
Pin Mill is the location for the annual Thames
barge race, but the barges here are stuck fast in
the mud and will never move again. They provide
homes for river dwellers. The small boats
belonging to local people lie haphazardly at low
tide. The stream to the left is a natural lead into
the quiet open foreshore. There are sufficient
warm colours on the hard to offset the prussian
blue of the barges where most of the detail is.

The Butt & Oyster : Pin Mill 20 x 14¼ in
For those who visit Pin Mill, if it's not the boats or scenery they come for, it's the pub. The Butt & Oyster occupies a commanding position in this landscape, at the end of the narrow lane off the road to Shotley Gate. At lunch time in the summer, you have no chance of a seat inside and just a slim chance of one outside.

This is one of my favourite paintings. Composed in the studio, it has miles of distance. An s-shaped lead in from the foreground boat takes the viewer through the shallow water, out and back towards the pub.
The white walls and red roof identify the building as the centre of interest. It is framed by dark trees providing plenty of tonal

counter-change. The rowing boats and groups of people are all carefully placed to make a satisfying composition with a lot of rich colour and atmosphere.
I especially like the weathered post and rope which hold the boat. I also like the pending rain shower which is going to ruin everybody's day.

88

Water's Edge: Pin Mill 19¼ x 12 in

Further along the river from the pub (opposite) is a small collection of buildings which I have painted many times, putting more and more drama into the subject each time. I have tried to give the impression of late afternoon sun at low tide. Note how the horizon is pitched high in the painting to accentuate the quiet expanse of reflecting mud. This area is a challenge. It is best handled with the simplest possible detail. Without the strong values for the background, the middle distance would have no sparkle to attract attention. The blue boat plays a support role, as a stopping point on the way.

This painting is a favourite of mine. It expresses not only what I felt about the location but also what I feel strongly about the watercolour medium. A watercolour should look good at a distance. It should have loosely applied colours and, most importantly, clean washes applied with clarity and minimal hesitation.

△ **Passing Shower** 19¾ x 13 in
Passing Shower is an imaginary location but a lot of the shapes come from Pin Mill. Again there is drama in the composition. Warm reeds set against cool water, warm buildings set against cool sky, white patches to grab the attention, boats at anchor with mast and rigging penetrating the sky, a happy combination of warm sunshine and imminent rain, a long, low horizon and a big sky. Put all these together, and with just minimal foreground details, the result is a painting with vibrant tones; pleasing to the eye. The foreground has a variety of lights and darks expected with a cloudy sky. The boats are placed, overlapping, one in front of the other, with a lot of light against dark throughout the painting.

90

Other river scenes

There are paintings from many different locations in this Section, but all include water either as lakes, rivers or streams. These subjects provide the opportunity to paint reflections, very discretely as in the painting opposite, or vigorously and with imagination as in *Going Fishing near Flatford Mill* (p.92). When I come down to my kitchen first thing in the morning and look out across the lake, I can tell what sort of day it is, just from the water's surface. How much wind, where it is coming from, how much cloud there is in the sky, whether it is raining, or if it has been cold enough to freeze overnight.

Likewise in a painting the water is a mirror of the scene; as in the calm of *The lake: Penn's in the Rocks* (p.95) and *The River at Batheastern* (p.96), or in the more vigorous painting of *By the Aberdovey* (p.97).

All the colours that are in the landscape and the sky will be required to paint the water, remembering the rule about tones; darks are painted lighter and lights painted darker. That is because some of the light entering the water is inevitably absorbed and fails to come back off the surface, especially if it is ruffled.

▷ **Mill Dale** 11 x 12½ in
This quiet stream was painted in front of the subject. My wife and I, out on a painting tour, located Mill Dale on the map and believed it might offer a good location. It turned out to be a disused iron works, but the river and immediate surroundings were ideal for a watercolour. A small bridge made a good place for my easel propped up against the stonework.
Mill Dale is a very simple subject, a steep wooded slope behind a stream. The trees and their reflections are mixes of prussian blue and lemon yellow. I especially liked the light on the trunks reflected up from the water. It is one of the few paintings in this book with vertical format.

P.B.CORNWELL

Autumn Colours: Bassetts Mill 12½ x 8¾
This is the view from our kitchen window; a small lake surrounded by oaks, beeches and birches. The bare trunks break up the background. The near bank is now cleared of alders and bull rushes which were beginning to encroach.
We see this view every day. It changes from bare branches to full leaf, then to autumn colour and there is almost always a good display with strong reflections.
For this painting the palette includes naples yellow, raw sienna and umbers with occasional greens from mixes with prussian blue.

Going Fishing near Flatford Mill 11 x 8 in
Flatford Mill and Lock is a centre for field studies on a tributary of the River Stour. The area around is recorded for posterity in many of Constable's paintings and if you know his work you can actually see them in today's landscape. One of his well-known works is *The Haywain* painted beside Willy Lot's cottage.
The house in my painting is that same cottage drawn from a different angle. I have set it amongst a background of trees with rushes occupying most of the water's edge. A couple of boys are trying to get their boat out for a day's fishing.
The bright dried rushes and the white walls are reflected in the river which has considerable movement. The subject is in strong light and has a certain mystery about it, not intended, but comes I think from the dark water and the deep shadows of the trees.

△ **The Ouse at Lewes** 20½ x 13¾ in
This sky with approaching rain was hastily laid in
first, giving the atmosphere for the rest of the
painting. Light was trying to break through onto
the group of cottages just where I needed it. The
impending rain is shown as vertical shading in
the clouds.

Here is a painting with a strong line along the
tops of the trees, roofs and chimneys. It has
foreground interest and distance. The bend in
the river, the slope down to the water and the
stone wall all provide subject interest.

93

The Lake: Penns in the Rocks: Groombridge 19¼ x 13¾ in
Penns in the Rocks is a garden open to the public just south of Groombridge. The lake is a major feature.

The strong horizontal lines in the water are painted against soft blue and yellow foliage. There are tall vertical trees in the far distance behind more gently rounded shapes. The conifers repeat the columns of the building. All this conveys tranquillity.

In the foreground the pattern of bare branches is accentuated by the light water. There is further counter-change, notably in the gazebo placed off-centre on the far bank. The small sapling on the extreme right has the important function of turning the eye round the corner of the lake back into the centre. The painting benefits from the simplicity of subject and the serene atmosphere of this location.

Upper Slaughter 14 x 9½ in
Of the two Slaughters, Upper and Lower, this one is the less popular but it has a quiet charm. In both, water runs through the village, but here in Upper Slaughter it is much overgrown. This end of the village is entered over a small bridge. I stood here and painted this picture over 20 years ago. I found the spot difficult to recognise when I went back recently. The area in front of the cottages is now dense trees and the stream almost indiscernible.

The cottages are of warm Cotswold stone with low garden walls. The strong reflections in the stream are loosely painted and very pleasing. This scene is only a short walk from Lower Slaughter (p.98) either by road or across the meadows.

Quiet Stream: Norton Marshes 11 x 8¼ in
This scene is on the Norfolk coast not far from those painted on p.16. Everything in the painting leads to the house. Small vertical brush strokes, in various tones, identify the coarse reeds along the banks of the stream. Note the way in which the light reflects off the duckweed which almost covers the surface.

The River at Batheastern 20 x 14 in

This village is about five miles north east of Bath. It sits beside a small river which runs south from the Cotswolds.

The scene offers one of the rare occasions when almost every line runs directly into the distance. The row of trees, the sides of the path, and the near and far banks place all the attention on the sunlit house and central tree. The other small building is enough to suggest that the river turns to the right.

I also painted this because of the autumn colour of the small chestnut trees on the left, among the first to turn, their leaves already falling around the seat.

Still reflections in the water indicate a windless day, the surface totally unruffled. The two fishermen in a small patch of light give just the right amount of human interest.

By the Aberdovey 21¾ x 14¼

This river scene has a very different atmosphere from the painting opposite. I am standing on the bridge just north of Machynlleth looking towards the river mouth. It is not unusual to find a local fisherman hoping for a catch. The current is taking the water over a rough bed providing surface lights as it races towards the sea. I have painted just enough detail in the opposite bank to suggest the constant erosion at this bend of the Dovey. The river is in a quiet rural setting, with considerable colour variation in the distant hills and in the sky. I liked the grassy field with its pattern of small trees and a patch of light running behind. It was this which first attracted me to paint this scene. The cows have stripped all the foliage off the trees up to head height.

The Covered Hay Rick 20 x 13¾ in
The two villages of Upper and Lower Slaughter are linked by the River Eye. It runs through lush pasture and enters Lower Slaughter to feed the old water mill. By the river is a path with a kissing-gate dedicated to the wedding of Prince Charles and the late Princess Diana. There, looking across the Eye, is a planting of young poplars, the location of this painting.

The detail which makes the trees interesting is the regular pattern of straight, upright trunks and open blue-grey foliage. My painting is just a small part of this woodland. A roughly built hayrick has been covered by a green tarpaulin, tied at the corners, but barely reaching the ground. I have broken its shape by a couple of trees close to the water's edge. I have also introduced some warmer colours in the hawthorn tree to make the silver-blues look even colder.

The edge of the river is boarded with old timbers. These and the trees give warm and cool reflections in the water.

Across Ullswater 8½ x 6½ in
This view towards Howtown on the east side of the lake is painted in very cool, muted colour with just a suggestion of warmth in the trees. The hard exposed ridge of the hills behind forms an interlocking pattern, directing interest towards the dark conifers on the bank.

There is a little movement in the water as indicated by the reflected darks and by the reflection of the white building at the water's edge.

In the Village: Lower Slaughter 13¾ x 10¼
This is one of the small bridges over the river in Lower Slaughter. They are all different.

It is a bright sunny morning with the light identifying the shapes of the Cotswold cottages, quite unlike the misty morning on p.59. I have used lots of colours in the water to describe the reflected sky (cobalt and cerulean blues with cadmium red) and the greens of the trees (lemon yellow in the distance). The bridge and the low fence are almost white paper with just small touches of reflected colour.

There is a pleasant feeling of warmth in this painting coming from the cottage walls and roofs complimented by the cooler foliage of the tree. There is also a sense of distance from the succession of roofs and the gentle bend in the river.

CORNWELL

By the River: Alfriston 18¾ x 12¾ in
The church at Alfriston appears in the painting on p.58. Here I wanted to capture the setting, the Cuckmere river and the shaded pathway that leads along the bank. The scene is painted against the light in various yellow-greens with strong blue-green shadows of the overhanging ash. Part way towards the church is a stile in a low fence, near the centre of the composition, inviting the viewer to explore. Cool greys in the distance provide recession, suggesting that there is quite a distance to walk before reaching the church painted in even lighter tones.

Conwy from Deganwy 13 x 9¾ in
Past the level crossing by Deganwy railway station the road bends along the edge of the Conwy estuary to give a good view of the castle and the new road bridge.
It was drizzling, so I opted to paint in the car, my stretched paper against the steering wheel, paints along the dash and my water jar outside. With the car door open I sketched the outline of the hills, masked out the buildings and roughly placed the small boats.
This is not the easiest way to paint watercolour but it is better than missing the opportunity altogether. I am not disappointed with the result. The painting has the right atmosphere, perhaps a bit more light than there was on the day, but I have the proportions of the bridge and castle about right and the small boats add colour to the scene.

Flowers & gardens

Wherever we have lived, my wife and I have always had a garden. This one at Bassetts Mill of about 11 acres has been developed from nothing. It is not all under cultivation but contains an extensive bog garden with free-flowing water all year round. This provides an opportunity for lush plantings of irises, primulas, hostas and other damp, shade-loving plants.

A garden for leisure purposes, as an extension of the house, has become of major interest to the British public. This is evidenced by the ever-increasing range of books, and radio and television programmes on the subject and by the number of new garden centres established each year. It is not that all people necessarily like gardening, but those who do take enormous pride in their own achievements and great interest in those of others. Our garden and the surrounding hedge rows provide subjects for a wealth of flower paintings, a well-defined craft in its own right. It involves separate skills and techniques at which my wife, as an oil painter, excels. Paintings of garden scenes combining soft plantings against architectural features, embracing the quiet atmosphere of garden terraces, have always been popular but no more so than today.

In this section I have developed a series of paintings from the simple window box (below) through more extravagant compositions of flowered balconies to hot Mediterranean scenes and tropical gardens.

◁ **The Window Box** 10¾ x 8½ in
A small gentle painting, the first of a series which helped develop the shop window paintings (p.50 & 51) and the balcony scenes (pp.106 & 107). Soon after painting this I also painted the stone sink at Castle Coombe (p.53), another offshoot of the series.
The *Window Box* is a still life of geraniums and other flowers, all softness and light, against the regular format of a window. Pale lemon-green foliage is set against dark reflections. The foreground leaves are further counter-changed against the overhanging sill. I had no subject in front of me for this painting. I was aware throughout of the need to handle it as an informal flower arrangement.

101

The Balcony 19¼ x 13¼ in

This is an extension of the previous painting. It was the first time I had tried to paint an elaborate, almost filigree, wrought iron balcony. I used a ruling pen with masking medium before painting began. The whole design was carefully measured out, believing that otherwise the overall effect would not be convincing.

Tall windows are set in a typical Georgian façade of warm stone. The lights and the strong darks in the window reflections come from the sky and surrounding shrubbery. White flowers and greenery frame the subject. Shadows beneath the balcony add some mystery to the ground floor. The lady has stepped out for a moment to enjoy the afternoon air.

I believe this is a successful painting developed from a simple idea. Along with the others in the series it was well-received at exhibition.

The Spiral Staircase 17½ x 13¾ in

This staircase also required drawing a lot of detail before painting began. The wrought iron work needed to be carefully explained, especially the shadows on the bottom steps, changing to shadows beneath the upper steps. The shadows rising up the wall, dark at the base and lighter towards the top, help describe the structure. With this very complex detail, everything else in the painting, a light and shadowy background of shrubs and a couple talking in the garden, had to be thrown away.

I would not wish to try this subject again.

△ **Herbaceous Border: Bassetts Mill Farmhouse**
20½ x 13½ in
Our herbaceous border starts the year with daffodils, irises and perennial geraniums. The sweet peas are planted in late April, before the delphiniums have grown too large, then tied repeatedly throughout the summer to wigwams of canes. At the end of the year colour is provided by dahlias planted wherever there is space.
This painting shows the sweet peas in full bloom against the background of hanging tiles and shrubbery. I have tried to capture the light on the flowers and the casement windows. It is the only one of my watercolours which hangs in the house, a reminder of what it will look like, hopefully, next summer.

△ **The Secret Garden** 18½ x 13½ in
A garden in the Cotswolds provides just
enough mix of architectural detail and foliage
for a painting; fleeting shadows across the
stonework, varied colours in the trees and
shrubs and low growing plants in full sun.

The steps through to the inner garden and
the small group of people there suggest quiet
privacy. It was this which attracted me to the
subject. Throughout the painting there are
considerable contrasts in tone which give
succession and vitality to what could

otherwise be a rather dull subject.
The wall and trees in shadow were important
in establishing the strongest darks in the
painting.

△ **The Long Hot Summer** 19½ x 13¼ in
This painting started with the balcony, the
wrought iron in darks (see p.102), and the rest of
the subject was built around it. The scene is
entirely fictitious. The girl's bicycle, the steps, the
open doorway, and the washing on the line all
raise questions. Who is this visitor and whom has
she come to see? No figure in the painting gives

an air of expectancy.
It is summer, the flowers are in full bloom and
the sun is providing mellow light across the
stonework. The painting employs strong reds,
yellows and umbers to emphasise the heat. The
bicycle is described just sufficiently to suggest it
has been hurriedly leant against the wall, waiting
for its owner to return.

Balcony of Flowers 18¼ x 14 in

The figure on the balcony seems to be awaiting a visitor. The colouring repeats the warm Mediterranean feeling of the painting opposite. The wide open louvered windows, the abundance of flowers and the washing hung up to dry all say the sun is up and it is going to be hot. Once again I have tried to create atmosphere in an imaginary location.

The chickens, bottom left, the figure above, and the steps down to the terracotta pots form a structured triangle. The walls and windows provide a soft background. The shutters, external wiring, the down pipes and the grille to the cellar all add to the ambience of the painting.

△ **The Trysting Place** 20 x 13¼ in
The Trysting Place is another imaginary
composition full of warm and cool colours. The
pair of white gates is a further exploration of the
techniques of painting filigree iron work, started
in the balcony series (p.102). The gates are off-
centre between two decorated brick piers but it is
not apparent what lies beyond. The eye is
therefore not tempted to explore, despite the
paved path leading up to the gates. Instead, the
action is kept this side of the wall between the

two small conifers and the pair of loosely painted
trees. But there is only one figure in the
painting - waiting for someone else?
This composition is again full of light against dark
and warm against cool, reversing the contrasts
where appropriate. It is this which gives so much
brightness in the painting. I was not sure what
the outcome would be when I started it, but, as
in many watercolours, a lot happens during the
painting process of which, at the time, one is not
completely in control and often not fully aware.

The Green Shade 19 x 13 in
Again a setting of flowers on a wrought iron balcony with delicate shapes and scrolls. All the interest is on the upper floor with its open louvered windows (as on p.106 & 107). A figure on the balcony is standing unobtrusively looking down into the square.

Below the attractive balconies is a rectangular shade keeping the sun off the shop windows. This is painted in viridian, hookers green light and cobalt blue, varying the wash as it catches the light. This contrasts with the curved red shade over the shop next door and takes the viewer by surprise in a painting of otherwise almost

uniform colouring.
There is borrowed colour from the shade in the lantern, on the woman's dress, on the left side of the balcony and in the door jambs below. All the wall colours are applied loosely to give the feeling of changing sunlight.

△ **Le Jardin de Balata: Martinique** 10¼ x 9½ in
The two paintings of this garden were developed from photographs I took some 15 years ago. I wanted to see if I could reproduce the luxuriant tropical atmosphere of the place.

The garden is private but open to the public. It sits high up on a mountain-side in central Martinique, close to an extinct volcano, often surrounded in mist and during my visit rain was dripping from every leaf.

There are exuberant palms and tree ferns typical of the West Indian rain forest. The whole area is characterised by juicy greens which I have tried to emphasise in both paintings. Beneath is a ground-cover of anthuriums, the national flower, lilies and other tropical plants. Divided palm fronds contrast with the large yellow leaf blades of bananas. The greens, mainly created from prussian blue, are set off against tiger lilies and the spathes of white arums.

110

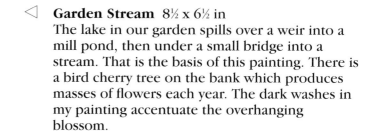

Garden Stream 8½ x 6½ in
The lake in our garden spills over a weir into a mill pond, then under a small bridge into a stream. That is the basis of this painting. There is a bird cherry tree on the bank which produces masses of flowers each year. The dark washes in my painting accentuate the overhanging blossom.

Agave: Elba 13 x 9½ in
This agave was growing by the road side in a mountain village among large round stones. It had vicious spines and probably grew so well because of that; no mountain goat would dare take a bite from it.
My painting shows the broad tough pointed leaves breaking the sky line almost like a group of charmed snakes. I have painted the agave against the light and used the shadows of the leaves to emphasise the smooth rounded boulders. The mountains and houses provide a simple background.

111

Sunflowers: Groombridge 20¾ x 13¾ in
Each year at Groombridge Place a few fields are planted with sunflowers. They are a show-stopper. As you come down the hill (p.41) into the village, the last thing you expect is this expanse of yellow.

It is impossible to stand in the middle of a field and paint sunflowers as a still life with an out-door background. Instead, I walked into the middle of the field and took a series of photographs, some in close-up, others distant to get material for a studio painting.

There is a lot of careful drawing in this painting. One or two flowers must be dominant, smaller ones giving support. They are all facing more or less in the same direction as they turn towards the sun.

Around the field are some large oak trees and I chose one for the centre background, some branches dark, others light. To show the flowers to advantage I used a strongly painted sky of cerulean, cobalt and ultramarine blues. The cottage provides the only straight lines of the painting.

112

P. B. CORNWELL

△ **Outside the Kitchen Window** 15 x 10¾ in
My easel is standing in the corner of this Suffolk
garden. The cottage faces south and gets most of
the sun. Of the patterns of light and shade on the
gable end the triangular shape across the window
is the key to the design.
Having painted that in some detail I decided to
simplify the rest of the painting, except for the

tree which I washed in loosely, concentrating on
form. The little wooden shed, bottom right, had a
lot of character. The clothes line did not exist but
the line and something on it was needed to
provide balance and a warm patch of colour. The
angle at which the blanket hangs is all important,
suggesting the slightest breeze.

113

Cotswold Garden: Lower Slaughter
21 x 13¾ in

The gardener who was tending his begonias let me take a photograph of his beautiful garden. I don't think I was the first to ask. It was full of colour and he was more than happy to agree. I would have liked him to be in the picture but by the time I was ready he had gone.

This is another painting in the wrought iron series. The composition is divided vertically by light on the cottages and the cool distant trees. It is also divided horizontally, about two thirds/one third, by the top of the stone wall.

The exciting detail is the garden gate. But it is the white fence which helps most in getting the viewer to go further and explore the distant cottages and small bridge.

I enjoyed painting this scene, especially the flowers and vines up the wall. I could not resist the twisted tops to the white railings.

Wild Flowers: Lanzarote 20 x 13¼ in

This subject is full of clear reflected light. Throughout the painting I had to mask out to achieve the glare coming back from the buildings, up off the field, from the white marguerites, and off the top of the low stone wall.

The buildings with their box-like shapes, low roofs and few windows are the main reason for the painting. The tower with the minaret is just off centre. The glare is made even stronger by the dark trees against the buildings and the shadows on the low wall (right).

The sky and hills are painted very simply. I reserved detail for the groups of flowers in the foreground. Here it was important to achieve the recession against the left hand wall. The field is full of pale washes of almost my entire palette. Blues and mauves are placed alongside yellows, pink shades, among earth colours and warm greys.

The painting succeeds in grasping the brilliant light of the Canary Islands.

Concert in the Park: Malvern 16¾ x 12½ in
How different this painting is from the previous
one. Here are strong blues, greens, ochres and
browns of an English town park. There is activity
in the trees and in the handling of the paint. I
want the viewer not only to see the bandsmen,
but to hear the music coming out of the painting.
Even the roof of the bandstand mimics the
cymbals clashing together in the opening chords.
Clashes in the painting come from putting the
pale cobalt blue roof against strong prussian blue
foliage and from the range of warm and cool
colours in the foreground. The square lines of the
municipal buildings and the abbey tower contrast
with the round bandstand. The briefly described
bandsmen in their red tunics really are enjoying
themselves.

116

◁ **The Lily Pool** 8½ x 6½ in
This small painting is full of light reflected from the lily pads, the shimmering water and the stone path. I have not described the water lilies in detail, but given just an impression of the way their rounded leaves float, tilting in different directions on the water's surface.
The hard diagonal line of the stonework is set against all the other less-defined forms in the painting. The path also provides the necessary balance of warm colours.

▷ **Summer Garden** 13 x 9¼ in
There is a very leisurely feeling to this painting. It is a very quiet place. A background of strong darks surrounds a sunny patch at the bottom of a garden. Detailed painting of the chair is set against very loose applications of colour behind. The lady's hat, the bottle and the newspaper on the chair identify a human presence. The terracotta pots and the yellow light coming through the fence, provide supporting interest for the table and chair. The blue umbrella suggests it is cool in the shade.

Red Hot Pokers 13 x 9½ in
I drove past this house and had to stop, go back, and take a longer look at it. Although the doorway was quite imposing, the house was really very ordinary. The curtains were part drawn and the house looked deserted. But whoever owned it clearly had a passion for red hot pokers, massed on both sides of the door. The wall in simple washes of light red provides a soft background for the cooler blue-greens.

The Tea Party 12½ x 9¾ in
Late afternoon sun is casting strong light on the side of this very old building near Kington in central Wales. Not only does the light identify character, the old slate roof, timber frame, and small windows, but it also sets up a pattern of colours and dappled light in the tree.
The patch of light in the foreground is a useful step towards the group of people having tea in the garden.

Old farm buildings

Every year passers-by knock on our door to enquire about "the Granary the dilapidated barn down the road. Who does it belong to and is it for sale?" It is admittedly falling down and very much in need of repair but buildings like this are fast disappearing and are of more than just sentimental value. They are an expression of the vernacular architecture of past times and built of many different materials depending on location. They are all infinitely preferable from a painter's point of view to the large open-sided concrete pillar and asbestos roof constructions of recent years.

These old farm buildings have served their purpose of housing animals, hay, grain and farm machinery. They are no longer economic to operate as part of the modern farm. They are often desperately in need of repair and at risk of ceasing to exist, becoming simply piles of stone and rubble for the demolition contractor.

Unfortunately the conversion of such buildings into homes often completely destroys their

◁ **The Broken Barn** 13¼ x 9¼ in

The Broken Barn is just a short walk up the lane from our gallery. It belongs to our neighbours who have threatened to restore it.

The painting is against the light, early in the year, while the sun is still low. The sunlit areas were first washed in with lemon yellow and cadmium yellow pale, avoiding the small sloping roof, the fence and some of the branches.

The winter trees were painted next in light red, burnt sienna and ultramarine, using neutral tint to vary the tones. These same colours appear in parts of the barn and the ground.

The shadows on the grass bank were dropped in without too much care; just enough to indicate where the light is coming from.

character in spite of restrictions imposed by local planning authorities. The best that can happen is that those worth restoring are taken apart and rebuilt This sometimes involves moving them to a new location where money is privately available to ensure their continued existence. The old farm buildings in this Section were painted in many different locations in their original landscapes

◁ **The Duck House: Alciston** 14 x 9¾ in
At the end of the lane in Alciston is an excellent view of the South Downs, especially Firle Beacon. Just there at the bend is a garden with a duck house, its bleached timbers contrasting with the dark stone wall behind.
Plenty of strong colour is used in this painting. The foreground, with rich tones and texture, is a tangle of weeds and wire netting. The ducks and netting were carefully protected with masking fluid before applying washes of pale blue-greens and cadmium orange. Some of these colours were also used in the field and downland.

▷ **Old Barns** 11¾ x 8¾ in
Rusted corrugated iron provides a very paintable building material for watercolours. The sheets often make up irregular patterns and light on the corrugations reflects an interesting textured surface. They are even better when contrasted with stone and slate, or, as in this painting, with the white rendered walls of the welsh cottages behind.
This farm is set against a steeply rising hillside covered with trees. The absence of a sky line makes the composition more compact.

△ **Oasts and Barns** 20¼ x 13½ in
This spring morning, with sunlight on the oasts and weathered barns, provides a typical Kentish scene. The sky and trees are a soft background to the roundels and staggered roofs. It is May, and the apple blossom is out, Kent farmers will be hoping for no late frosts to ruin the crop.

Here is a lot of detail; the glass house, fence and gate. There is an old cart and tractor by the barn door where two locals are chatting. The muddy duck pond is full of shadows and reflections. All this presents a very rural scene which can still be found.

121

Bend in the Road: Foolow 17¾ x 12 in
Foolow is in Derbyshire, a mile or so from Eyam.
Here the plague, the Black Death, was contained
by self-imposed quarantine in 1665. This is the
area of the Derbyshire peaks, of sheep, low stone
walls and few trees. It is not far from Hucklow
Edge (see p.149).

The Bend in the Road: Foolow shows typical
small Derbyshire farm buildings in direct sunlight
surrounded by a warm blue-grey sky and nearby
trees. The sun is making strong shadows across
the road as it turns away to the left, inviting the
viewer to explore round the bend.

Spring at Milton Street 10¼ x 7¼ in
When the stems of young willows begin to turn
yellow, spring is not far behind. The buds just
beginning to break give a golden-yellow sheen to
the trees. They stand out in the landscape whilst
all else seems still in winter.
This is what I have painted at Milton Street just
across the fields from Alfriston. The tops of the
willows are merged into a warm grey sky of
cobalt blue muted with neutral tint. Their light
trunks are emphasised against horizontal colour
in the buildings. This gives an almost chequered
effect and adds interest to the painting, especially
with the reversal of dark roofs and light-toned
walls.

Farm Buildings near Lewes 12½ x 9½ in
The colours in this painting are a little
warmer than in the one above, but the
treatment of the subject is similar with
enough breaks in the sky to let the sun
through.
The trees are still bare except for some
autumn leaves still hanging on. Descriptive
lighting on the roofs and chimneys helps
model their shapes. The mixture of warm
blues, browns, greys and yellows combine to
create a pleasing atmosphere of a very rural
scene.

123

Chiddingstone Oasts 18 x 12½ in
Many oasts in Kent have been converted into
homes and the number of farms growing hops is
much reduced. Most of the conversions have
been done sympathetically but I prefer to paint
oast houses as they were, without their newly
acquired windows.

Here a dark brooding sky of cumulus cloud
overshadows the oasts and trees, highlighting the
roundels and producing a strong dramatic
atmosphere. Backlighting of the clouds is
responsible for sunlight getting to the distant
hills. The simple treatment of the foreground
accentuates the oasts as the main subject.

After Rain: North Wales 11½ x 8½ in
Strong sky tones again provide unusual lighting
in the landscape. Fleeting sun catches the tops of
the trees through a momentary gap in the clouds.
Within minutes the light has gone, it has poured
with rain and then the sun is fully out again.
The cottages are in light behind a large calm area
where a few sheep are grazing. The lane bends
out of the picture but instinctively we know it will
turn back to the house. The white wall steals
almost all the attention.

Pembrokeshire Farmstead 11½ x 8 in
To make a successful painting there has to be
something about the subject, you may not know
quite what, which makes you want to stand there
and get it on paper. Here I think it is the
patchwork of fields, trees and farm buildings. The
hills and clouds blend, so that you are not quite
certain where one begins and the other ends.

△ **Kentish Oasts** 20½ x 13½ in
This joyful explosion of colour says "winter is passed and spring is here". The trees with delicate blossoms, out in flower before their leaves, allow the shapes of the oasts to filter through.
The effects in this picture are achieved by the loose painting of the blossom against the sky, the resulting hard and soft edges to the buildings, and the contrast of soft foreground trees against the tall upright poplars behind.
The painting has a lot of fluid edges and pleasing contrasts of tone and colour. The dark, very simple foreground ensures that the fallen blossom adds to the enjoyment of the painting.

Behind the Barn 14¼ x 10 in
This old farm building with its rusty corrugated iron roof, crumbling stonework and broken timbers is probably used as a hay barn.

The painting has two main areas; the fence and pole on the left which lie in the picture plane and the barn itself which recedes up a slight slope. The two provide an interesting composition with the foreground remaining as a quiet sunlit area.

I think I agree with the lady who now owns this painting when she said: "I do like old farm buildings that have not been tidied up too much".

Oaks: Sussex Farm 13½ x 9¾ in
These old farm buildings are a couple of miles south of Groombridge, painted as much for the oaks coming into leaf as the barns. Oaks have an easily recognised rounded structure and here I had the added bonus of good branch shadows cast across the trunks. I used yellow ochre for the foliage, touched with light red, and mixtures of ultramarine for the branches.

The barns are casually placed, the furthest built off the ground with a short flight of steps. They are described in various blues mixed with yellow ochre and light red. The foreground is painted in full sunlight under an open sky.

127

△ **Derbyshire Cottages** 14¾ x 10¼ in
A group of walkers has just come up the lane through the hollow made by the high bank on the left and the stone wall. They have now reached the top in the sunlight. The tree shadows in the foreground draw attention to the walkers.
The painting has good atmosphere helped by the breezy sky and the leafless tree. There is something a little gaunt about the buildings. This is emphasised by the low sun.

▷ **Stone-Walled Cottages: Derbyshire** 13 x 9 in
The atmosphere in this painting is similar to that in *Derbyshire Cottages* (above). But a little more sunshine, and thus some clear yellow, is lighting the fields, warming the farm buildings and brightening this otherwise sombre scene. Cobalt blue is washed into the foreground puddles. The clouds and tree on the left suggest quite a wind blowing, a good drying day for the washing hanging on the line.

◁ **Evening Light: Derbyshire** 11¼ x 8 in
The paintings on this page are a pair .Some of the farms in Derbyshire are isolated and become remote in poor weather. I wanted to portray the bleak conditions of the Derbyshire Peaks.

This painting enjoys a lot of light on the buildings. Pale washes of cool colour, prussian blue and raw sienna, help model one barn against another, offering just enough detail. The difference in their shape and size is emphasised by the dark sky and the group of trees. Strong light on the fields is again only briefly described. The gates indicate the way up to the farm.

◁ **Derbyshire Farm near Foolow** 11¼ x 8 in
This painting combines ultramarine and light red to achieve much warmer effects. It has a strong sky line of trees, roofs and chimneys. The granulation in the sky is encouraged by admixture of the ultramarine with a touch of raw sienna. The stone wall crossing the farm track creates a triangle of light in front of the buildings.

P. B. CORNWELL

◁ **Towards Aber Falls** 9¾ x 7¼ in
A very limited palette of just three
colours, prussian blue, raw sienna and
burnt sienna, provides the feeling of a
wet cloudy day on this walk up to the
falls. The Welsh farm is painted simply
but strongly against the distant hills
with sunlight across a sloping
foreground.

△ **Suffolk Farmhouse** 16 x 12 in
Here is the front of the farmhouse in the painting
Outside the Kitchen Window (p.113). It is a lively
composition with a great deal of sunlight in the
trees and around the pond. The house is detailed
only at the gable end with a tracery of shadows
and light across the window. I especially like the
stone wall and fence which looks in need of
repair.

The South Downs

The Downs of Kent and Sussex are major features in the English landscape. The South Downs begin in Hampshire and continue towards Chichester and Arundel. They eventually reach the sea at Brighton and culminate in Beachy Head. The coast line from Seaford Head to Eastbourne incorporates a magnificent view of the cliffs from Birling Gap (p.27). This stretch of the coast is known as the Sussex Heritage Coast. Its character must be preserved.

Because chalk is a soft porous rock, what would otherwise have been steep scarps and slopes have been weathered into gently rounded shapes. These I have painted with care to ensure that particular locations, like Firle Beacon, are easily recognisable.

The Downs have long been used for grazing sheep and there is a well-established market at Hailsham set in the middle of the sheep-rearing district. The famous Southdown sheep of this area are now widely established around the world. They were first bred at Glynde, in about 1770, just a few miles from Lewes. I have included sheep in a number of my paintings. The landscape would look empty without them.

▽ **Towards the South Downs I** 12 x 8¼ in
A summer landscape full of sunshine and warm colours painted at harvest-time near Arlington.
The whole sky was put down in one application with some extra darks dropped in top left while the wash was still wet. These suggest a little back-lighting to the clouds directed onto the farm buildings.
There is no detail in the barns, just typical Sussex shapes. The dark trees behind help create space between the farm and the Downs. The foreground with simply described stubble occupies about one third of the painting. This helps create distance.

△ **Towards the South Downs II** 20½ x 14 in
Gentle light in the late afternoon creates a calm
peaceful scene across open fields. The sky looks
as though it is going to take a little while to clear,
but light is beginning to brighten the middle
distance with the Downs still in shadow. The
darks in the foreground make the trees, the
rough pasture and the sheep come forward.
Hedges surrounding the fields were carefully
described with those furthest away less detailed.
As a result, the painting has miles of distance, an
effect helped by carefully registering the tones
and running warm to cool towards the Downs.
The low horizon and big sky enhance this effect.

132

Sheep Grazing under Willows 21½ x 14½ in

A lot of atmosphere achieved with a narrow range of colours. Bright fields are set against a darker sky which gives the impression of a still, almost thundery afternoon.

The landscape bends round by the willows towards a small group of sheep in a calm area of the painting. This contrasts with the area of long grass which is full of activity but not distracting. The trees are painted openly with a lot of sky visible through the branches, a feature characteristic of pollarded willows. The smaller trees on the horizon keep the viewer within the picture frame. It is a calm, restful composition giving an impression of space.

P.B.CORNWELL

▽ **The South Downs at Alciston** 20½ 13½ in
Sketches and a small watercolour of the shape of
the quarry provided the reference material for
this painting. An enormous amount of human
energy has gone into creating this large chalk pit.
The painting reproduced here emphasises the
scale of it. It is a very powerful subject. This effect
could only be achieved by coming up close and
reducing the scene to a bold statement.
Washes of cobalt blue and pale yellow ochre were
allowed to take up their own positions in the sky,
without encouragement. The white of the chalk,
pure white paper ,was paramount in emphasising
the concave shape with the minimum of detail.
The warm trees at the base, diminutive in scale,
draw the eye unhesitatingly to the subject.

P.B. CORNWELL

△ **Firle Beacon** 19 x 11¾ in
A very different painting from the one opposite.
No part of it seeks overriding attention. Strong
sunlight and shadow in the sky create lively
movement in the landscape.
This area of the Downs is so well known that it
was vital to get the shapes right. For instance,
the way Firle Beacon rises very gently before
dropping sharply to the west is familiar to many.
Furthermore, in a painting of sunlight and
shadow it is important to have a sky which is full
of colours and tones which produce a varied
landscape without competing with it. That
balance is not always easy to achieve.   135

P. B. CORNWELL.

High and Over: the Downs near Alfriston
24½ x 19 in

I went out with a sketch book and a few colours to get the details for this painting. I scrambled up a bank opposite the scene and made some drawings and colour notes. These I put together the same day in the studio to produce this painting, a series of gently flowing shapes from the flat top of the Downs to the valley bottom which leads up to Alfriston.

The Downs do not offer much by way of colour in early spring. The painting is more about the rounded shapes gently flattening into horizontal lines. These I put in with a loaded brush pulled against a straight edge, wetting the bottom to let them run. In spring the Downs are also short of detail, but perhaps it is that which gives this painting some appeal.

Cow Parsley on the South Downs 20¼ x 14 in

The white flowers of cow parsley, or 'Queen Anne's Lace' as they are often called, border our country lanes every spring. But more attractive are the dried umbels, seeds of the flat-topped inflorescence, holding fast to their stalks well into late autumn. Seen in silhouette these miniature umbrellas look very appealing against a clear sky. That is what I have painted here with the South Downs behind.

The background was first washed in with pale mixtures of cobalt blue and raw sienna, suggesting distance. The graded sky gives the impression of summer haze. I used burnt sienna for the stalks and seed heads leaving some parts unpainted to pick up the light. Cow parsley often grows up through a mass of vegetation which is best understated.

137

Fields & hillsides

▽ **Fordcombe Meadows** 20 x 13 in

This landscape is the flood plain of the River Medway. Here the meadows are usually cut for hay and the fields then used to graze sheep.

The strong horizontal lines make this painting very calm. The hazy sky and open fields suggest a warm sunny afternoon. These old willows are often buffeted by strong winds and there are a lot fewer now than there used to be. I have painted this scene many times, trying on each occasion to record the effects of season on the landscape (see p.82). In early summer it is universally green, but here now, later in the year, autumn colours are beginning to appear. The expanse of dried grass is painted without detail except for the merest suggestion of some stubble.

◁ **Rooftops at Cley** 12¼ x 9 in
Inland from Cley, towards Wiverton, the sails of the windmill can be seen above the rooftops with the magnificent Cley church to the east. The artist is spoiled for choice.

On this warm afternoon I chose the mill and rooftops under a clear sky. The houses are all different shapes and make an interesting skyline. I kept the foreground very simple, textured with a few tufts of grass.

▽ **Towards East Bergholt from Flatford Mill** 12½ x 9¼ in
The church at East Bergholt features in Constable's paintings. He was born in this village just over a mile from Flatford Mill, once owned by his father.

You can see the Church of St. Mary the Virgin across the fields, the rectangular tower standing proud of the trees. Apparently its 15th century builders ran out of money and never completed the tower. The bells are still in a wooden cage in the churchyard. Sunlight is breaking through the clouds, highlighting the church and surrounding fields; a simple subject, made interesting by the drama in the sky.

This final section of the book includes some of my sky paintings. If the landscape is painted simply and without too much detail, panoramic scenes provide the right subjects for loose, dramatic skies.

One of the important requirements in a cloudy sky is a sense of perspective, the impression that the sky is rising up and going over your head, with the clouds getting smaller and less detailed towards the horizon. It is equally important to observe the sequence of blues from the top of the painting down to the horizon, often warmer in the distance and therefore muted to a warmer grey.

Fields and hillsides also provide good subjects for a cloudless sky, which needs a graded wash to suggest a heat haze over open fields. There is an example on the previous page and in *Malvern Hills from the West* (p.143). Long shadows across fields tell the time of day as in *Late Afternoon Bury St. Edmunds* (p.148). There are different effects at noon, with the fields in full sun as in *Roof tops at Cley* (p.139).

The English landscape is often admired by visitors from overseas for its pattern of small fields enclosed by hedgerows, as in *Towards Eridge* (p.143). In this scene clear sunlight throughout the painting provides a ready made opportunity to paint distance, as the fields get smaller further away and the hedges less well defined. The painting of *Suffolk Landscape* (p.141) is yet one more example of "aerial perspective", a strong lead into the painting reinforced by strong blues to identify distant trees.

P.B.CORNWELL.

△ **Late September: Suffolk** 19¾ x 13¾ in
My wife and I were driving from Lavenham to
Norwich on a very hot summer's day. Mile after
mile of cornfields were there for the painting,
some already harvested. We broke the journey
and drove into a narrow lane. A gap in the
hedge gave me the location I was looking for.

An hour and a half was sufficient for a quarter
imperial watercolour which hung in our house
for a long time. The half imperial painting
reproduced here, *Late September: Suffolk*, is an
elaboration of that small watercolour.
The subject is typical of the low horizons and
big skies so often seen in Suffolk and Norfolk.

The central trees and farm house are the
principal subjects. The one minute sky washed
in with the minimum of effort provides just the
right atmosphere for the fields of stubble in the
foreground.

140

Suffolk Landscape 15 x 11½ in
Another Suffolk scene with a wide open sky, put in very loosely with the washes allowed to intermix on the paper. "Put it on and leave it alone" is the best possible advice to achieve these effects. The strong line of trees on the horizon in prussian blue emphasises the warmth in the cornfields. The lane and foreground trees are an encouragement to walk into the painting to investigate the farm buildings grouped in bright sunlight. The painting evokes the flat open countryside of Suffolk.

141

△ **Brecon Beacons** 18 x 11½ in
The Brecon Beacons are the highest mountains
in South Wales inside the National Park. This
painting is a small section of a much wider
landscape.
Excitement in the painting comes from the
vigorous use of colour, especially the light in the
sky, painted in hookers green light, directed
towards the landscape. The central area of warm
light grabs attention. In front is a group of
weathered boulders which have come to rest in a
rough terrain of gorse and heathers.

142

Malvern Hills from the West 11½ x 8½ in
Here is another group of hills with easily
recognised shapes. They run in a line from east of
Ledbury in the direction of Worcester.
I set up my easel at ten o'clock in the morning
waiting for the sun to break through on top of
the hills. They were quite hazy, but about ten
minutes into the painting all that had gone, to
leave a well-defined ridge against a graded sky.
The east side of the hills has Great Malvern and,
in season, the Three Counties Show. The west
side is very different. It gets more rain, is more
undulating and has more varied trees. Conifers
are grouped around the houses which, half-
hidden in the landscape, give the scene an almost
Italian atmosphere.

Towards Eridge 14 x 10¼ in
Early spring sunshine is lighting this small
scene of fields and trees. The sun is
modelling the oaks by the house and casting
long shadows on the hedgerows. The eye
follows the criss-cross pattern of fields
through to the distance.
Leaves are not yet fully open so there are still
mauve tones among the branches. But on
the horizon the sun is producing warmer
colours which stand out against the graded
sky.
Just a few colours and a few square inches of
watercolour paper encapsulate a glimpse of
typically English countryside.

143

△ **Gills Lap : Ashdown** 19¼ x 13¾ in
Gills Lap is almost the highest point on
Ashdown Forest, now better described as
heathland since the forest has gone. On this
small rise there are distant views towards East
Grinstead and the North Downs. It has a
trigonometrical point. Christopher Robin and
Pooh made excursions here.

Whenever I paint this scene I want to add
something extra to the group of trees which
contain a rainbow of colours, to the sun-dried
grass, heathers and gorse, which now make up
most of the vegetation, and importantly, to the
sky from where all the light and much colour is
coming. This makes the painting vibrant and
exciting. There is a place to park at Gills Lap, to
get out and walk along a well-worn, rough track
across to the trees. It is there that you discover
the dry sandy soil, at least in Summer, and
wonder how the short scrubby vegetation
survives.

Towards Ashdown from above Hartfield

12½ x 9 in

Ashdown sits on the top of an anticline, the Weald. Here layers of different rocks, sandstones, clays and chalk, have been eroded to expose a succession of soil types from north to south. This has had considerable influence on the streams, rivers and vegetation of the area.

In this painting we are on farmland, mainly clay. Hartfield Village has a variety of old and new properties from the 16th century onwards, and was the home of A.A. Milne and the Christopher Robin stories.

Again it is the clouds which provide shadows on the landscape, the farm buildings and the trees in the middle distance. Light on the immediate foreground identifies the lines of stubble in the cornfield creating a strong perspective into this brightly lit subject.

The Cornfield 18½ x 13 in

The colours in this imaginary scene set in a hot climate describe an open courtyard. The buildings, especially their shutters, suggest strong, almost vertical light. As a result, the cornfield taking centre stage is broadly lit and the trees are in part light and part shade. The people are placed to draw attention to the cornfield and the lavender haze behind. The two small trees, incongruously on the horizon, almost at right angles to it, emphasise the strong horizontal. Cold blues are used to paint the foliage, cerulean and prussian. These are interplayed with viridian, hookers green dark and lemon yellow. There are also touches of cadmium orange in the leaves and on the ground. The tree colours are repeated in the shutters, adding to the illusion that these are to keep the building cool.

146

Summer Meadows 20¼ x 13 in

An English landscape with all the attributes of a warm summer sky, fleeting clouds, gently rounded, almost manicured trees, flowers in the meadow and cows grazing in the field. What more heartening scene could you wish to wake up to?

There is a wide palette of warm colours set against cool to give vibrancy. The spacing of the trees provides an important gap in the centre. Note too how the trees lean slightly outwards to contain this broad scene within the frame.

Low sunlight is just catching the right-hand side of the trees and putting the left in strong shadow. Notice how this gives the obvious counter-change in the two trees close together.

Long shadows under the trees produce an almost continuous band of cool colour. It emphasises both the sunlit field behind and light in the foreground which I have painted with movement as the breeze stirs the long grass. The flowers are briefly hinted at.

△ **Late Afternoon near Bury St. Edmunds**
19¼ x 13 in
Contrary to normal practice, darker trees are painted against an already dark sky and the distant landscape, already light, against a light sky. Normal procedure however is resumed in placing the sunlit steeple against the darkest clouds and you will also discover further examples of normal counter-change in other parts of the painting. All this helps create distance. The sky colours are repeated on the ground, mixtures of prussian blue with umbers and raw sienna. The lines in the field are just a final touch to break up this area and involve the viewer in the subject.

This is a studio painting produced from a small watercolour on the road.

B. Cornwell

Towards Hucklow Edge: Derbyshire
19½ x 12½ in
The main advantage of the car that I drove some
years ago was its very low boot and low roof. This
meant that I could put my board with its
stretched paper on the boot lid and dispense
with an easel. I could also lay out my colours and
look over the top of the car to paint. They don't
make that model any more.
So standing there on a rather chilly day I painted
Towards Hucklow Edge, an open landscape of
fields and stone walls, distant trees and cumulus
cloud.

Where the wall is in shadow I painted the
stonework in warm washes, picking out
occasional details. But where it is in light, on the
left, only the capping stones are described. The
shadow on the road is a device to get the viewer
on to the road and then into the landscape. I like
the occasional patch of sunlight on the distant
ridge and the three-dimensional clouds low on
the horizon. My son, who worked for some years
underground in Derbyshire, knows this area well,
and has this painting hanging on his wall.

Corner of the Wheatfield 12¾ x 9¼ in
Strength of colour is so important in a watercolour where sunlight is a major feature. The bales of straw are the principal subject here, with crisp geometrical shapes in an otherwise soft late summer landscape. I needed those hard edges as a foil against the other dark shapes in the painting. I wasn't going to risk painting the bales without first masking out.
Now imagine this painting with no dark trees at the end of the field, or the shadow created by the big tree at the side. There would be nothing. No brilliant sunlight, no interesting shapes of the straw bales, no atmosphere to say "this is a hot summer's day".

October Mists 20¾ x 13¼ in
Morning mist often hangs in the landscape until the sun has just enough power to dissolve it. Then almost by magic the landscape, previously obscured, comes into focus. This painting attempts to record those few moments when the first colours appear. The trees and fields at the edges of the painting have begun to emerge, while the centre is still hazy.
This subject requires muted colours. It needs careful use of lost and found edges to give the impression of detail seen in the mind but not actually on the paper.

P.B.CORNWELL

△ **Snow over Burrswood: Groombridge**
21½ x 14 in
Burrswood was founded by the late Dorothy
Kerin as a healing centre. She built the church of
Christ the Healer using local village builders. It is
situated in attractive countryside just a few miles
from our gallery. We could see Burrswood from
our previous house in Groombridge before we
came to Bassetts Mill.
On this cold December day, snow is still falling
with just a suggestion of weak sunlight. But there
is still a lot more snow to come.

151